THE WORK I DID

THE WORK I DID

A Memoir of the Secretary to Goebbels

Brunhilde Pomsel
Thore D. Hansen

Translated by Shaun Whiteside

The biographical part of this book is based on conversations
with Brunhilde Pomsel that were recorded in Munich for the
film *Ein Deutsches Leben (A German Life)*

BLOOMSBURY PUBLISHING
LONDON · OXFORD · NEW YORK · NEW DELHI · SYDNEY

Bloomsbury Publishing
An imprint of Bloomsbury Publishing Plc

50 Bedford Square
London
WC1B 3DP
UK

1385 Broadway
New York
NY 10018
USA

www.bloomsbury.com

BLOOMSBURY and the Diana logo are trademarks of Bloomsbury Publishing Plc

First published in 2017 in Germany as *Ein Deutsches Leben*
by Europa Verlag CmbH & Co. KG Berlin . Munchen . Zurich . Wien

First published in Great Britain 2018

Copyright © 2017 Europa Verlag CmbH & Co. KG Berlin . Munchen . Zurich . Wien
English translation © 2018 by Shaun Whiteside

British Library Cataloguing-in-Publication Data
A catalogue record for this book is available from the British Library.

Library of Congress Cataloguing-in-Publication data has been applied for.

ISBN: HB: 978-1-4088-9449-1
TPB: 978-1-4088-9448-4
EPUB: 978-1-4088-9447-7

2 4 6 8 10 9 7 5 3 1

Typeset by Newgen KnowledgeWorks Pvt. Ltd., Chennai, India
Printed and bound in Great Britain by CPI Group (UK) Ltd, Croydon CR0 4YY

To find out more about our authors and books visit www.bloomsbury.com.
Here you will find extracts, author interviews, details of forthcoming
events and the option to sign up for our newsletters.

CONTENTS

Is it a bad thing, is it egoism, if people try to do something in the place where they have been put, that is good for them, and they know: I won't be harming anyone else?

But who does that? No one thinks so far ahead.

We were short-sighted and indifferent.

Brunhilde Pomsel, Munich 2013

The Work I Did *is not only one of the most important contributions to the analysis of the Holocaust, but in view of the current political situation a long-overdue, timeless warning to present and future generations.*

Daniel Chanoch, Holocaust survivor

FOREWORD

Thore D. Hansen

As a shorthand typist and secretary to Joseph Goebbels, Brunhilde Pomsel was close to one of the biggest criminals in history. Shortly after Adolf Hitler seized power, Pomsel briefly joined the Nazi Party in order to get a job with Reichsrundfunk, the Reich Broadcasting Corporation. In 1942 she switched to Hitler's Ministry of Popular Enlightenment and Propaganda, finding herself mixing with the elite of National Socialism. In the last days of the war, when Soviet troops were already in the streets of Berlin, she was still typing out legal documents and even sewing the flag for the official capitulation of Berlin rather than grabbing an opportunity to flee. She remained silent about her experiences for over seven decades.

In their documentary film *A German Life*, the film-makers Christian Krönes, Olaf S. Müller, Roland Schrotthofer and Florian Weigensamer put Brunhilde Pomsel in front of the camera and allowed her, in impressively lit black-and-white pictures, to tell stories from her life. Her narrative is both disconcerting and fascinating. This book is based on the memories she recorded in 2013. They were arranged chronologically by the author, and carefully corrected where spoken language and grammar required it.

Brunhilde Pomsel's account begins with her childhood in Berlin, where she was born in 1911. It covers the outbreak of the First World War and life with her laconic father, who returned uninjured from Russia in 1918, as well as the strict upbringing that she received as the elder sister of four brothers, and which had a lasting effect on her. Her father was an uncommunicative man, and politics wasn't discussed at home. She grew up in one of the more affluent parts of Berlin and the family could feed itself comparatively well, while in the rest of Berlin, as in Germany generally, wide sections of the population were suffering. The country was subject to unrest: the politically extreme opposites – Communists and National Socialists – protested on the streets, and there were increasingly violent clashes. But in the Berlin district of Südende, a part of the city with numerous villas, there was little sense of the conflict.

In retrospect, Pomsel's indifference towards the new Nazi Party strikes her as crucial for her career. Heinz, her summer romance, introduced her to a decorated officer from the First World War. That meeting was to be fateful for the young woman. The officer in question was Wulf Bley, later a radio reporter and early Party member, who took her under his wing – the man who, as a reporter, would use overblown language to describe the torchlight procession after the victory of the Nazi Party in March 1933. Shortly after Hitler came to power, he took Brunhilde to the Deutsches Theater, where Bley, the author manqué, was failing as a dramatist. In the end, as a member of the Nazi Party, he was offered a job with the Reichsrundfunk and told Pomsel to join the Party so that she could be his secretary. The corporation had been cleansed by the Nazis long before, and all the Jewish directors had been dismissed and banned from employment.

Only a short time later, Wulf Bley was moved again, but for Brunhilde the meeting with him was the start of a social ascent that would take her to the inner circle of power – the beginning of an extraordinary era. While she has lost many memories in the intervening seventy years, central events and turning points remain vivid in her mind. The details and the way she deals with her experiences in the Reichsrundfunk and later in the Ministry of Propaganda are not free from considerable contradictions. Again and again we come upon passages where she withholds something only to admit it elsewhere – and this makes her narrative fascinating.

Brunhilde Pomsel's story does not give us fresh historical perspectives. But it gives us insights into what it was like for a person caught up in those times, and so warns all of us in our own time. It is almost indisputable that now – as then – we find ourselves in a political situation where anti-democratic tendencies and right-wing populism are gaining ground again. Political and sociological analyses have been actively engaging with the question of how it can be that it is socially acceptable in Europe and the United States to express right-wing ideas, to scapegoat whole groups and tolerate attacks on minorities such as war refugees.

Brunhilde Pomsel wasn't interested in politics. Her job came first, along with her material security, her feeling of duty towards her superiors, and the need to belong. She describes her career vividly and intimately. She denies any personal responsibility for the crimes of the National Socialist system. But after the premieres of the film *A German Life* in Israel and

San Francisco there were very few scornful voices or attributions of blame. 'Hats off to anyone who could confidently claim he wouldn't have joined in,' as the correspondent of the *Frankfurter Rundschau* put it.

Rather than provoking a condemnation of Pomsel's life, the documentary prompted questions about our time. Are the dark 1930s being repeated? Are our fear, ignorance and passivity in the end responsible for the strengthening of the new right? For a few decades we assumed that the ghost of fascism had been exorcised. But Pomsel makes clear to us that this isn't so. In the film, her amazingly clear accounts of her harmless everyday life in the middle of wartime, her rise as an 'apolitical girl' and her emotional detachment from reality are mutely juxtaposed with Goebbels quotations, mountains of corpses and the skeletal figures of Jews who were sent to the concentration camps.

The comparisons with the present day inspired me to juxtapose Pomsel's experiences with recent developments and make them my theme. Are fears that history might repeat itself exaggerated? Or did we reach a point long ago where a new era of fascism or authoritarianism can no longer be prevented? Can Pomsel's story give us clues about the extent to which seeking personal advantage allows us to be ignorant about social and political developments?

The challenges of the modern age in the form of digitisation, financial crises, wars, waves of refugees, climate change, the social parameters of a networked world and the resulting fears of decline and rising immigration have led to many people withdrawing into the private sphere. Seventy years ago Brunhilde Pomsel lived in a time completely different from our own. She tells us of her small decisions, which at first strike the listener as logical, reasonable and understandable, to the point where every individual can wonder: might I too not suddenly have found myself sitting in Goebbels's outer office? How much of Pomsel is there in each of us? Or as one editor asked provocatively after the premiere of the film: 'Are we not all Pomsel to some extent?'

And millions of Pomsels, who only think of their own advancement and material security, and at the same time put up with injustice in society and discrimination against others, are a solid basis for every manipulative, authoritarian system. And this makes them more dangerous than the radical hard core of voters for extremist parties. In the end, Brunhilde Pomsel had to watch her country drag an entire continent into the abyss.

Engagement with the parallels between past and present allows us to adjust our own moral compass so finely that we notice when we have reached the point where we need to take a position, stand up and confront things clearly and openly. How casually do we treat our inner moral measuring instrument? For what primitive, short-term, banal and superficial goals or apparent successes do we sacrifice this inner standard? These are questions to which the story of Brunhilde Pomsel cannot and will not provide any universal answers. Only individual willingness to reflect can do this.

In many European countries populists are on the rise. The leaders of some European countries, such as Poland and Hungary, are already dismantling democratic systems. Not to mention Turkey, where the principles of the constitutional state and freedom of opinion have already lost their validity and where mass arrests and purges of supposed critics have become the mechanisms of an emerging dictatorship. And it might not be the last.

And then there is the phenomenon of Donald Trump in the United States, with the dirtiest election campaign in US history against minorities and migrants, as well as against the establishment. An election campaign waged with lies and racist slogans, which enabled the property mogul to reach the office of President. By mobilising voters with slogans and simplistic solutions in a highly complex world, Trump became the 45th President of the United States – yet over 40 per cent of the US population did not even vote.

Are these the harbingers of a new age of authoritarianism that threatens the very foundations of freedom and democracy? Against this background, Brunhilde Pomsel's story serves to confront the reader with the urgent issue of our own responsibility for contemporary events – as a warning to stop looking away.

On the pages that follow Brunhilde Pomsel tells us of her childhood, her work to the end of the war, her subsequent internment in a Soviet special camp and her return to freedom. Also running through her biography is the fate of her Jewish friend Eva Löwenthal, who at first was able to keep her head above water in Berlin as a journalist, but was finally deported in 1943 to Auschwitz concentration camp, where she was murdered.

Pomsel's story reveals a lack of interest in politics among the population, along with a loss of empathy and solidarity: one of the causes for the rise and success of the National

Socialists, even if she herself does not or cannot see this in a way free of contradictions. She allows us a glimpse into ourselves. And reminds us of the words of the Polish author Andrzej Stasiuk: 'The more afraid we voters are, the bigger the cowards we elect. And these administrators of fear then sacrifice everything to remain in power: us, our country, our continent of Europe.'

Thore D. Hansen

January 2017

Before 1933 nobody thought about the Jews anyway; it was all invented by the Nazis later on. It was only National Socialism that made us aware that they were different people. Later that was all part of the planned programme for the extermination of the Jews. We had nothing against Jews.

Brunhilde Pomsel

'WE WEREN'T INTERESTED IN POLITICS': GROWING UP IN 1930s BERLIN

Brunhilde Pomsel's memories begin vaguely, with the outbreak of the First World War in August 1914, when she is three years old. Her mother receives an unexpected telegram, and her father is one of the first to be called up for military service. They take a fast coach to Potsdamer Bahnhof to say goodbye to him. After four years of war, Brunhilde's father comes home unharmed in November 1918.

My memories are very important to me. And they pursue me, too. They won't let go of me. I may forget names and certain events that I can't describe in words. But otherwise everything is there, as if in a big encyclopedia or a picture book. I think back to when I was a little girl. And I know that in my life I have given a lot of people joy by my very existence. That's a lovely thought too.

When my father came back from the war, I very clearly remember us asking our mother, '*Mutti*, what's that strange man doing in our flat?' And then a difficult time began. We were living from hand to mouth in those days. Towards the end of the First World War, soup kitchens were set up. Even though my mother always cooked and prepared everything for us, at one point she said, 'Let's try them out,' and she took us children to one of those soup kitchens and we had lunch. And when we left she said, 'I'm never doing that again.'

On the way home I told my mother: 'I'd like to bang in a nail for Hindenburg.'[1] There was a huge wooden figure in Königsplatz, a crude depiction of Field Marshal Hindenburg. And for five pfennigs – a *Sechser*, Berliners called a five-pfennig piece a *Sechser* – they handed you a hammer and a nail and you were allowed to knock the nail in somewhere, at a particular spot. That was... you had to do that. She donated the money to make me happy.

My father had been lucky. He was in Russia, always in Russia, and yet he wasn't injured, let alone killed. But the war had marked him in a different way. He had become an even quieter man than before, and perhaps that was why politics was never discussed at home. Until the Nazis came, and then it was, but even then only superficially.

Things weren't easy for big families in those days. There were five of us children. Then they wanted to have another girl, but they got only boys. Such matters were out of your control in those days, so it was all left up to chance. As the oldest and the only girl I was a bit overstretched. I was responsible for everything the boys did. It was always: 'You should have kept an eye on them!' By my standards today children back then weren't brought up well enough. Children were there, and they were looked after, and they ate their fill, and to a certain extent they were given toys, a ball or a doll, but no more than that. We had to ask for everything and were brought up very strictly. We were smacked every now and again. We were a really normal German family.

So as the eldest I carried certain burdens around with me. And even when you grew up a bit later on and had some wishes or notions, there was always a bit of malice in the response, along the lines of: Yes, yes – you ask for so much. You weren't taken very seriously. We lived very modestly, but we always had enough to eat. I can't remember being hungry or anything like that, and that wasn't something you could take for granted when there were armies of poor and unemployed people.

Our father ruled over everything, and we asked him for a lot of things that we often tried in vain to get out of Mama, but she wouldn't fall for it. Mostly she said, 'Ask Papa!' Later he became a good friend, but when we were little we had to do as we were told. We learned what we were allowed to do and what we weren't. And we were punished for doing things we were not allowed to do. There were many such things. For example, every now and again precious apples were bought. Then they lay in a fruit bowl on the sideboard, and everybody knew how many there were. Suddenly an apple was missing. 'Who was it, who took the apple? Nobody? Everybody come in here! You, you?' Everyone was questioned individually, but not me. 'Right, so if it wasn't anybody there will be no apples any more.' Then you could say, 'I saw Gerhard playing around with the fruit bowl.' So the children were played off against each other.

Or again, my mother had the habit of putting small change in a cup in the kitchen cupboard. It was very tempting to reach in and take out a 10- or 20-pfennig coin. Someone did that once and gave himself away by suddenly running about with a huge stick of rock. Children are very stupid. These things were punished to set an example. And then we got a smack on the backside with the carpet beater. That hurt, I can tell you. And after that there was peace in the family again, my father was happy that he had done his duty, and we children didn't think it was so bad that we wouldn't consider doing it again.

Obedience became a part of family life; love and understanding didn't get you very far. Obedience and a bit of cheating, fibbing or shifting the blame on to someone else were also involved. So characteristics were brought out in the children that weren't necessarily part of their nature. Love wasn't the only prevailing emotion among the many people living together in a flat. We all got what was coming to us. That was perhaps less true for me as a girl, but I often heard: 'As the biggest one you should have known.' So I was forever having disappointment rubbed in my face. I was always responsible for everything the boys got up to.

When we were ten or eleven years old, we always wanted to know how our parents had voted. They never told us. Even today I don't know why. It was a secret. Politics wasn't something we talked about at home. We weren't interested in it. My father was quite secretive anyway, not least about his youth. He too came from a big family. And much later, long after his death, I learned that his father had taken his life. And that my father had grown up in Dresden with his brothers and his only sister in an orphanage. I found that out by chance only about forty years ago. My mother was still alive at the time. I asked my mother, 'Mama, didn't you know?' And she said, 'Yes.' And

I asked her, 'And why didn't you tell us?' 'Papa didn't want me to.' Papa didn't want her to, so she didn't.

His father had been a court gardener at the Saxon Royal Court; he even had a title. He bred a strawberry and got a diploma for it, and also a considerable sum of money. Anyway, he went on to speculate on the Amsterdam flower market and lost all of his property, a very nice house with a garden, and then abandoned his wife and five children by jumping off a bridge in front of a train in Dresden. A tragedy that troubled my father a lot. We weren't supposed to know about it, but I learned of it from a cousin many, many years later.

I remember constantly hearing that we had no money. Papa was a decorator and had a job, and that in itself was a luxury in those days. So we always had enough. We almost never went hungry, unlike so many other people after we lost the First World War. There was always something to eat. It was simple and plain, but it filled you up. A lot of vegetables. My mother made wonderful vegetable stews; I sometimes long for them even today. Whether it was Savoy cabbage or white cabbage with caraway or green beans with tomatoes, it was a real luxury. And we still had enough for a goose at Christmas, which we just had to have. And Papa had to have his little glass of beer too. And Mama always got something nice to wear for Easter.

When I was about fourteen, my friends were getting suits or coats. I wasn't. I got hand-me-downs, which were altered for me. They were made to fit, and I wasn't exactly spoilt. I knew we didn't have very much money, and if you got something everyone else would want it as well – that was the principle. They were always talking about how there wasn't any money, but we could always pay our rent, and when I'd finished compulsory education and the teacher said, 'The child absolutely has to go to a higher school, she's gifted,' money was spent on that as well. So my mother got money out of my father for middle school. And I stayed there for a year. Then that was the end of middle school. If you wanted to do the *Abitur* you had to go to the Lyzeum.² That was out of the question. Studying? Who studied ninety years ago? Only a very select group. Not us, anyway.

When I was still at school I wanted to be an opera singer or a teacher. I was such a good pupil that a rich lady asked my mother, 'Frau Pomsel, couldn't your daughter do her homework at our house, with my Ilse? I can't do it, and she's not making any progress; she needs support.'

Ilse was a friend of mine, and I was happy to do it. We did our homework together, which isn't to say that I let her copy from me; I really helped her and explained things to her. She made considerable improvement, just because I was patient with her and liked going there. They were a very wealthy family. I always got a cup of coffee or tea straight away, and of course there were cakes as well, and the mother was an Italian, a former opera singer. They also had a wonderful piano, and she always sang – she sang us opera arias, and we sat there entranced and listened. It was a lovely time, and it was better for me too, because it was always noisy and busy in our flat. I could never do my homework in peace. And I wanted to become an opera singer, but there wasn't enough money for that.

And then at our middle school you could also attend a housekeeping school. But my father said, 'That's enough: I'm not paying for that as well. She'll learn housekeeping at home, not at school. School's over.' So after my first-year exams I left middle school.

At first I stayed with my mother as an assistant housekeeper. But that didn't work. It was terrible. I couldn't stand working in the kitchen, and Mama was relieved to send me off around the flat dusting, because I got everything wrong in the kitchen anyway, so it was all a terrible disappointment. My mother always wanted me to do a proper apprenticeship. But at the time I just wanted to work in an office, it didn't matter where, it just had to be an office. For me the ladies who worked in offices – secretaries, office managers or business representatives with an insurance company – were very attractive, and that struck me as something definitely worth striving for.

And then I found myself a job in the *Berliner Morgenpost*, which already existed back then: 'Hard-working young female volunteer wanted for two years.' I took a closer look: Hausvogteiplatz. That was a very smart area at the time. I knew that was where the upper class of the country lived, a posh area. I was to present myself at one o'clock. I immediately got on the train and travelled to the firm of Kurt Gläsinger and Co., which was on Mohrenstrasse. It was all very elegant: an amazing house with red carpets and a lift. I went up the stairs, which had soft carpets. I stepped inside a very beautiful big office, and there sat Herr Bernblum, a Jewish confidential clerk, severe, but a real personality. And there were three or four ladies sitting there. One of them was reaching the end of her contract. He gave me a good going-over. He asked this and that, and suddenly he said, 'Yes, fine – here's your volunteer's contract. I just need one of your parents to sign it, since you're still underage. Can you come back with your father or your mother?'

I went home in great excitement and told my family straight away. I got a terrible telling-off at first: 'The impudence of it, without asking, and who paid your fare?' But then Mama came with me and signed a two-year contract, for the princely volunteer income of twenty-five marks a month.

Then I did everything that needed to be done at Kurt Gläsinger and Co.: shorthand, typing, and in the evening I took courses at business school and learned the basics of bookkeeping. But at Gläsinger's they didn't need my knowledge of shorthand, which would later enable me to get into broadcasting and the Ministry of Propaganda. Even before my internship I was brilliant at shorthand; I was always first to finish, only because at school I was in love with my teacher. But he wasn't in love with me.

I worked there for two years. The best bit was always the journey to work. I took the suburban train from Südende to Potsdamer Ringbahnhof. Then I had to walk to Leipziger Platz. That was always a half-hour walk. And if I went via Leipziger Strasse rather than Mohrenstrasse I passed by lots of lovely shops. Wonderful fashion shops with unattainably beautiful things. But it was always lovely to see the clothes and dream.

And the business, the daily work itself, was good fun as well. I learned everything properly, like a good girl, and probably made quite a good job of it. By the end I was even allowed to go on telephone duty. We had even had a telephone at home for some time – strictly forbidden to us children. We weren't allowed near it. Who would we have called? We had no idea who you would have called. Who had a telephone in those days? Now Herr Bernblum said to me, 'Fräulein Pomsel, put me through to Schulze and Menge.' Then, as he watched, I had to find the number, my hands shaking, and then they would answer: 'Südring exchange.' And then I would say, 'Please put me through to the Nordring exchange.' And then someone else would answer, 'Which number?' Then I would say the number, and eventually the company would answer. And then I had to say again, 'I would like to speak to Herr So-and-so, for Herr So-and-so.' That was difficult for someone who had never done anything like that before. You can hardly imagine. These days it's hard for me to cope with a mobile phone.

But I was very industrious back then. I always was. I always was. It's stayed in me. That very Prussian thing, that sense of duty. And a bit of self-subordination. It started in the family; you had to fit in or else it wouldn't have worked. In those days there was always an element of strictness to everything; it meant you had to ask for everything, and you had no money at your disposal. There was no pocket money back then, like there is today, when children get pocket money from their parents from a certain age. We did get something. Well, I only got something because I had done the washing-up at midday every day, for the whole family. That wasn't so easy in those days, not like just turning on the tap and rinsing the dishes. I had to heat up heavy pans, and then we had two basins: one in which you did the washing-up with soda, and a rinsing basin and then a drainer. It involved a lot of work. And I also got pocket money for that. I even think it was two marks a month. That was why the transition to the internship and my first money was very important for me.

I stayed with Herr Bernblum for two years. After that they asked me to stay – for ninety marks a month. I had to discuss that with my parents because I wasn't yet twenty-one. And my father said: 'Ninety – no that's not enough. You must ask for a hundred!' And the next day I told Herr Bernblum my father insisted on a hundred. 'I'm sorry, then – we'll have to fire you.' And then they fired me. My father said, 'Quite right; find something else.'

So I went to the labour exchange for the first time, registered as unemployed and was given a list of addresses where I was to go and present myself. For a short time I ended up in a bookshop. I absolutely loved reading. I hadn't yet read very much, but reading was absolutely lovely, and they also paid the hundred marks without objection. It was that bitter cold winter of 1929, and by then I was eighteen years old. But it was a terrible job. They didn't turn the heating on until very late, and the staff were cliquish and very unfriendly. I was desperately unhappy there.

But then my father met a neighbour of ours in the street, Herr Doktor Hugo Goldberg, a Jewish insurance agent, and he talked to my father – 'How are you; how's business; what are the children up to?' And eventually my father said, 'Hilde's grown up, and she's working already.' 'So, what's she doing?' Then Herr Goldberg said, 'You know what? My secretary's about to get married, so she'll have to stop working anyway. Send your daughter along to me, she always was a very clever girl.'

So the next day I went to see Herr Doktor Goldberg at his house and introduced myself to him. I'd never seen him before and I greeted him with a curtsy and everything. So then he says, 'Let's give it a go. The world of insurance is very interesting. You can't know everything, but you'll learn a lot.' And then I started working for him in the middle of 1929.

After that came a calm and lovely time. For the first two years they often had parties at Herr Goldberg's. They were all people with a lot of money. He lived on a huge floor of the villa. I remember a party for his wife's fiftieth birthday. It was all supposed to happen against a medieval backdrop, and he had bought everything he needed for it. He used my father for the construction of the stalls; he helped him a lot. And when it was all finished, he said to my father, 'We could use your daughter here as an orphan boy.' I knew lots of his friends and acquaintances from the telephone. When my father asked me I immediately said yes. So I showed up as an orphan boy. The guests were all Jewish friends. Dr Goldberg was always having these fantastic ideas. Anyway, the party started in the late afternoon and lasted all night, and I was there until the morning. I had short trousers on and a little jacket with a feather on it, and I had my boots over my shoulder. It was wonderful.

Over time I learned a lot about the insurance business there. There was always a lot of dodgy dealing going on – but still, there was a lot of money left over. Except not for me. I was getting ninety marks there again; that was the usual price for office girls at the time, but over the four years that I was there, in my last year, 1932, I went up to a hundred and twenty marks. Then, just before 1933, Dr Goldberg cut my working time by half, as his business wasn't going so well. By then I had the feeling that he would soon be closing up his office and his flat in Germany. From then on I was only there from eight in the morning until one in the afternoon. And he had no money left and was very poor.

At the time I had a boyfriend – Heinz, a student from Heidelberg. Not a great passion, but he was my first boyfriend. My girlfriends all had boyfriends already who they would meet up with, and I didn't have one. We all went to a tea dance, and they had brought him along, and we were paired off. He had hardly any money because his father kept him very short of funds, because he didn't want him to study but to take over the firm. And I had nothing either. Of the little that I had, I handed some over at home, even if it was only five marks. So there was very little left for me. And when I met Heinz, we actually only went walking. He didn't take me to the cinema, because he would have had to pay. And I couldn't have taken him out, because it wasn't done in those days. When we went for a coffee, he had to pay. That was how it was; I would have insulted him if I'd said no. And anyway it wouldn't have occurred to me. When you went for a meal or a cup of coffee or whatever with a man, he had to pay. It didn't matter what he did or got in return. Crazy, all the rules in those days that you just unquestioningly obeyed.

Then, and this was still before 1933, my boyfriend Heinz had two tickets for the Sportpalast, which was always an event in Berlin. Boxing matches, and then those wonderful skating displays that were typical of the Sportpalast. So I went with him. I was looking forward to it, because I didn't know what to expect.

He was waiting for me with a crowd of foul-smelling men, who were all sitting on benches and waiting for something. And we waited too. Suddenly there was music: a band, which played an exciting march. That was all very nice too, and then came a fat man in uniform – Hermann Göring. He delivered a speech that didn't interest me at all. Politics. And why would it have done? I was a woman, and I didn't need it. Afterwards I just said to Heinz, 'Never make me go to anything like that again. It was incredibly boring.' Then he said confidently, 'I thought the same.' He didn't even try to persuade me that a party had been set up that would free Germany of the Jews, nothing like that.

Before 1933 nobody thought about the Jews anyway; it was all invented by the Nazis later on. It was only National Socialism that made us aware that they were different people. Later that was all part of the planned programme for the extermination of the Jews. We had nothing against Jews. On the contrary: my father was very glad to have some Jewish customers, because they had the most money and always paid well. We played with the children of the Jews. There was one girl, Hilde – she was nice. And next door I remember a Jewish child my age, and I played with him sometimes, and then there was Rosa Lehmann Oppenheimer with her little soap business; I remember her too. So it never occurred to us that there was anything wrong with them. When we were growing up, nothing at all. And when National Socialism came closer and closer, we still didn't understand what might come. And we waved at our beloved Führer. And why not? First people wanted work and money. We had lost everything in the war, and the Versailles Treaty defrauded us, we were later taught.

None of us had any idea what was coming our way with Hitler.

Brunhilde Pomsel carries on with her carefree life, not guessing that she will soon take a job in the centre of power of the National Socialist dictatorship, which will change her life for ever.

For my friend Heinz, I was too stupid for politics, too immature. But there was no reason for us to fight about it. I just had somebody I could meet on Sundays. We would go somewhere on the S-Bahn, take a stroll, have a coffee, and afterwards go to his flat. It was very nice that we were able to be alone at last. Afterwards I often went to see my friends. Yes, I had friends. The boys were each more handsome than the next. One had a motorbike, and riding out of Berlin on the motorbike, into the surrounding area, that was an experience. It was all very harmless. But among themselves the boys were sometimes political, and we girls weren't interested, we didn't even listen. There was one who was a member of the KPD: the German Communist Party. He was still handsome. We liked him anyway. The others were certainly all Nazis or German nationalists.

Sometimes I think, should I reproach myself for not having been interested in politics in those days? On the contrary, perhaps it was a good thing. Perhaps in youthful idealism you might have even found yourself on one side rather than another, and then you could have been killed. In those days I was easily influenced, but I had a different circle of friends. They weren't all Nazis by any means: they were rich people's sons, slumming it a little. None of them had jobs – they were about to go to university, or not. Their parents could afford it at least; most of them were big business people. They had their villas in Berlin-Südende, their sons were between about twenty and twenty-three, and none of them had thought about taking a job back then, or at least not so quickly. They were just bumming around really. They were my friends. Handsome boys, nice boys that you would have been pleased to meet. There were always these lovely occasions: parties, student parties. All the *Gymnasien* had some kind of anniversary party every year. They were often held in the Parkrestaurant in Südende. That was a wonderful meeting place for things like that in Berlin, by a lake, with a bit of forest around it, and rowing boats or dinghies.

In the winter it was usually covered with ice, and then they turned it into a skating rink. And they had this wonderful giant restaurant and a lovely party house, for big dances and smaller events. And even if you barely had any money for a beer, twenty pfennigs was enough, and then we drank together. The main thing was that we were sitting together in a pub. None of those young people was interested in politics. Not one. But of course there wasn't a single Jew in the clique. Only my Jewish friend Eva Löwenthal, she was often there.

Politics was largely uninteresting as far as we were concerned. When I see what schoolgirls get up to today, expressing their opinions and everything, I think to myself: my God, that's a difference; that's an incredible difference. Then I sometimes think: I'm not over a hundred years old, I'm three hundred years old. Their whole way of life is completely different.

In late 1932 Brunhilde Pomsel meets the future radio announcer Wulf Bley. It is a crucial meeting that, after Adolf Hitler's seizure of power, will smooth her path into broadcasting and later into Joseph Goebbels's Ministry of Propaganda. The author and radio announcer Wulf Bley (b.1890 in Berlin; d.1961 in Darmstadt) joined the NSDAP (Nazi Party) and the Sturmabteilung (SA), the paramilitary arm of the Nazi Party, in 1931. Bley was known to posterity chiefly for his observations about Hitler's seizure of power, when on the evening of 30 January 1933 he commentated on the torch-lit procession of the National Socialists through the Brandenburg Gate and later on parts of the 1936 Olympic Games.

Anyway, my boyfriend Heinz had an acquaintance – a writer, a flight lieutenant from the First World War. Heinz knew that I was going to have to halve my hours of work for the Jew Dr Goldberg. Heinz's acquaintance wanted to write his memoirs and needed someone to type them up for him, and Heinz suggested that I write to him. And that was Wulf Bley, a very nice, friendly man, who didn't live far away from us; he had a terribly nice wife and a nice son. When I turned up there was coffee and a bit of a chat. And then I put his thoughts down on paper. And it went on like that. Herr Bley had a friend, Captain Busch. He lived in Berlin-Lichterfelde. He wanted to write his memoirs as well, and could I perhaps help? He was very generous. So I went there every day and worked until dinnertime. Then one of his sons would drive me home. They had a lot of money, and he almost made me rich. And so at the end of 1932 I was working for the Jewish Dr Goldberg in the morning, and on some afternoons for the Nazi Wulf Bley. I was sometimes asked if I didn't think it was a bit reckless, working for a Nazi and a Jew? No. At the time I was at least one of the ones who still had a job. There were huge numbers of unemployed in those days. Almost all my friends were unemployed. And I had been with Dr Goldberg for four years; that was lovely. That was before 1933. But then all at once everything changed.

It was all a bit ambivalent. But I didn't feel it was all that serious. I was completely uninterested in those things. At the time I was a young girl in love — that was what mattered to me. And it's all so long ago. I can't see things from that perspective any more. That's simply how it was in those days — you just slipped into it.

Brunhilde Pomsel

'HITLER WAS SIMPLY JUST A NEW MAN': JOINING THE REICHSRUNDFUNK

At the end of 1932 Brunhilde Pomsel is twenty-one years old, and under the laws of the time she has reached maturity.

Berlin was a vibrant and open city, and had a lot to offer. Of course, that was only for people who had money. For the rich Jews. For the people who had money, there was a lot in Berlin. It was a city that had everything. It had things that people considered important at the time: theatre, concerts, a wonderful zoo. There were also lovely big cinemas too. There was always a film, then there was a film about culture as a B-feature and a stage show, often a solo singer and a man at the piano, or a dance revue, the Tiller Girls. There were lots of things like that. Everything people needed. What else could you want? There were very smart restaurants, expensive restaurants, and of course mortal feet never stepped inside them. I only found out a bit about that when I started at the radio station.

But while Berlin might have been praised to the skies, it had always had its dark sides, and particularly then, after losing the First World War. Unemployed people on every corner, beggars, poor people. Anyone who lived in good areas, as I did, in a good suburb, didn't see any of that. Of course there were particular areas swarming with poverty and wretchedness; you didn't want to see things like that, you just looked away.

Then in March 1933 the Nazis suddenly won the elections. I don't know how my parents voted. I can barely remember how I voted. German National Party, I think. The colours were black, white and red. I always quite liked that as a flag. Even in childhood election Sundays were different from normal Sundays. There was an atmosphere with flags and posters and life all over Berlin. Election days were really fantastic. But it was about politics... So, we young people weren't involved with it at all. And we weren't influenced.

A short time before, in January 1933, my boyfriend Heinz dragged me along to Potsdam, where Hindenburg, an old man by then, and Hitler shook hands. I didn't even ask what that nonsense was all about. I didn't even want to know. And he noticed how stupid I was, how uninterested in politics. I certainly wasn't worthy of him. And he didn't try to convert me either. The Party wasn't an issue between us at all, and within the year we split up anyway.

When Hitler was appointed Chancellor in January, the whole of Berlin was on its feet. The really mad ones made the pilgrimage to the Brandenburg Gate. And of course my boyfriend Heinz made the pilgrimage too. With me. All I remember is Hitler standing at the window of the Chancellery. People, people, people everywhere, roaring as they would at a football match these days. We roared along. And when you'd roared and cheered enough, the others jostled you out of the

way, and then you were delighted to have witnessed a historical event. I was one of the ones who cheered. It's true, and
I admit it. Hitler was simply just a new man.

But I certainly wasn't enthusiastic. I could never get enthusiastic about that. Later, I tried to avoid gatherings like that if at all
possible. I mostly managed to do that. I remember later, when
I started working at the Reich Broadcasting Corporation, we
always had to march to the Reich sports field or to Tempelhof
airport, when Mussolini came and so on. Then we had to put
in an appearance. There were certain people in the departments that you didn't really trust – who whispered things to
somebody or other if you didn't join in. They kept a close eye
on who didn't come. But we weren't stupid either. We went
along nicely and marched along a little way. Then, when the
big march began – I remember one time, it was a march to the
Reich sports field – we had to meet in front of the broadcasting
building. But our department had arranged to meet in a pub.
Every five minutes or so one of us crept away from the march
and went to drink a beer instead. Of twenty people, only two
ever showed their faces on the sports field. But that was always
a small risk. There were certain departments that were kept
under particularly close surveillance. For example, the literature department of the Broadcasting Corporation.

But immediately after Hitler's accession, the mood was
simply one of new hope. It was still a huge surprise that Hitler
had done it. I think they were surprised themselves. But I was
so uninterested at the time. For me, life just went on. I was
still working for Dr Goldberg as well. Of course, I hadn't told
him that I had cheered Hitler on 30 January. I didn't do that;

I was still tactful enough not to do that to the poor Jew. Such things weren't done. It was all a bit ambivalent. But I didn't feel it was all that serious. I was completely uninterested in those things. At the time I was a young girl in love – that was what mattered to me. And it's all so long ago. I can't see things from that perspective any more. That's simply how it was in those days – you just slipped into it.

We weren't all that aware of the Nazis' parades and torch-light processions either. Südende was the rather smarter part of Steglitz. We didn't know anything about the uprisings either in the 1920s or later, when things got going with Hitler. Everything was very nice and middle class. You found those things more in the parts of the city where the workers lived. Berlin Südende, where I lived, was a very smart part of town, and a few very well-off people lived there; there were a few very lovely villas and big houses where whole floors were rented out, and there were the shops and business people you would have expected. And there was a certain harmony there. I don't think I saw a single procession in Südende. They just didn't have things like that, and no one would have taken part. Certainly not there. And we didn't go to other places. There were a lot of things in the paper, but it was all very peaceful where we were. We had a certain flair. Those riots were on the main street, on Steglitzer Strasse, and then there were Nazi processions. You got out pretty quickly. In fact it barely touched us. The fact that my brothers joined the *Jungvolk* and wore those brown shirts – well, that was just how it was.

And then more and more SA were running around in the streets. They didn't bother us, though; we didn't give them so much as a thought. And there was also a Nazi Women's League, although I was terrified that they would introduce a law that said we all had to join. There were rules about what you had to wear. BDM – Bund Deutscher Mädel – they had to wear blue pleated skirts. My whole circle thought they were dreadful. We wore tight skirts at the time: that was the fashion, and they were running about in this strange kind of clothes. That was really what worried me at the time. I managed to get out of joining the Nazi Women's League. I can't remember how I did that. There was no compulsion, but they did their best to drum up membership. I didn't want to join a mass movement; I've always rejected that.

But after Hitler came to power, all the rules and restrictions got going, and a lot of things changed very quickly. Suddenly there were a lot of regulations, including emergency regulations. But there was also a lot that was positive: they started building the Autobahn – that was a huge change, and it kept people off the street, because among those beggars and poor people there were a lot who were hanging around out of real poverty, not because they enjoyed bumming around and idling. They were unemployed, and had too little support for their families, most of which were growing. Wherever there were poor people they had fewer children than the rich people did. Overcoming the consequences of the First World War that had been imposed on us: Hitler got to grips with that very well at first.

At the time, some young people felt that this was a liberation. My brothers could go and sit in a pub in the evening, which they had never done before. They joined the Hitler Youth and were with their peers away from home. They went wherever they felt like; they went on outings, away from their parents. At any rate there were so many things that were suddenly better. So that you just had to say: my word, this is all fantastic.

Then a little while later – I hadn't quite finished doing Wulf Bley's book with him, and immediately after the 1933 elections he was called to the Deutsches Theater as a dramatist. He suggested I came with him, and that was the beginning of my rise. Without the lucky chance of meeting Wulf Bley, my whole life would probably have taken a different course and I'd have ended up somewhere else as a secretary. And he said to me, 'Well, your Jewish boss won't be around for much longer. Don't you fancy working for the Broadcasting Corporation? I'll find something to dictate to you.'

I still remember that he'd told me that before, in about Christmas 1932: 'So, these National Socialists – another election and they'll have done it.' And if they'd done it, he would be sorted out for the rest of his life. And that was what happened. He had belonged to the Party even before. Not even the clever Nazis knew that a completely fake, completely unartistic person was being given a job in the Deutsches Theater. But he got the job shortly after Hitler's seizure of power.

They were just rehearsing their first big theatrical performance at the time: *Wilhelm Tell*, with Heinrich George[1] as Gessler and Attila Hörbiger[2] as Tell. I sat around in the theatre and had nothing to do at first. Every now and again he would dictate some letters to me. But he valued me so much that he always paid me a slightly bigger salary. I was glad of that, and I enjoyed it. Particularly when the secretary – the theatre secretary, one Fräulein von Blankenstein – allowed me to visit her in her office. On one wall she had portraits of all the actors hanging up with a dedication. One of the greatest things was when I was having a conversation with her and the door opened, and who comes in? The actor Attila Hörbiger, who was every girl's heart-throb at the time. He took out a cigarette case and offered me a cigarette, which I smoked, trembling. Those were experiences that I regaled the dinner table with in the evening.

A few months later Herr Bley told me he was going to negotiate with the Broadcasting Corporation, and he asked me if I would be interested in taking a job there. He could bring his secretary, but he wanted her to be paid by the Broadcasting Corporation, rather than paying her himself. He wanted to get me a contract with the Broadcasting Corporation. That's great, I thought, with such a big company. What an opportunity! So I was very happy to say yes.

A short time later he said to me: 'It looks like it's working; it looks like it's working. With you too. I think we can bank on it.' We were still going to the Deutsches Theater, where he still had his job as dramatist.

Then he said a little while later: 'You are in the Party, aren't you?' 'No,' I said, 'I'm not in the Party.' 'Hmmm,' he said. 'It would be a good idea to join, for a company like this.' 'Well,' I said, 'then I'll join.' 'Yes,' he said. 'I don't know if it's open for membership at the moment.'

At that point the Party was *the* Party, and the whole world wanted to be a member. Because everyone assumed that this would be the big man who was going to be on the side of the little people. This had been their message before, so it was a good idea to belong to the Party. And I thought I'd join too, as he said it meant I could work for the Broadcasting Corporation. And then I told them at home, 'I'm going to join the Party, for this or that reason.' Well, my parents didn't care either way – 'Do what you like.'

And that same afternoon my Jewish friend Eva Löwenthal paid me a visit, and we were going for coffee. That actually meant taking Eva out for coffee, because we all knew she had no money. If you said, 'Let's go for a coffee', it meant 'I'm taking you out for coffee.' So I said: 'Eva, we can't today – I have to join the Party very quickly!' Because the Party always opened up, let a few hundred or thousand people in, and then closed again. They couldn't keep up with making the membership cards, so people had to queue up again until it was their turn with the next recruitment drive.

'Yes,' Eva said, 'I'll come with you.' Eva and I went together to the local group in Südende. There was an NSDAP there, and at least a hundred people were standing outside. They all wanted to join the Party because they thought it would be closed again on the first of the month, and it was a good idea to be in.

I had to join the queue. While she waited, Eva sat on a wall. And it all happened very quickly; it was very well organised. You went in and you had to sign something. The monthly fee was supposed to be two marks – that was painful, that was a very big sum. But even more painful was the fact that I had to pay a ten-mark joining fee. That was harsh. That was my whole kitty. It meant going for coffee was out of the question. Ten marks was a lot of money at the time.

But I signed anyway, because I thought that if things worked out with the Broadcasting Corporation, I'd forget the ten marks very soon. And things did work out, so I joined the Party. Later, if anyone asked me, 'Are you in the Party?' I said, 'Yes, I'm in the Party.' But otherwise no one actually asked me. And later, when I was working in the Ministry of Propaganda, no one asked me at all. I don't even know if they were all in the Party. So that was an over-hasty move on my part, but it didn't do me any harm either.

Then, after a few weeks, I got a letter from the local group and a proper membership card: member of the NSDAP since such and such a date. Then I got another letter, because, they said at the time, as a member of the Party you had to do something for the Party. You had to take part in street collections, and they had a few suggestions. Then I thought: let's wait for a while. There were street collections all the time, the tins were always rattling for all kinds of things. I didn't yet feel that I was affected. But then I got a letter telling me to report to the local group.

So I went along and they made it quite clear to me that I was now a member of the Party and I hadn't yet done anything for the Party. 'Right, what am I supposed to do?' I asked. 'What do you do for a living?' 'I work for the Broadcasting Corporation.' Right, they said, then I could write for them in the Party office. At six in the evening when the shops were just closed, they had a bit of mail to sort out and needed someone to write.

So I no longer had an excuse, and had to type out pointless things. Then I phoned them and came up with some excuses.

I can't come: we've got a programme this evening and I have to be there. They believed me. The next week I had a different excuse until in the end they said they were no longer interested in me working for them since they couldn't rely on me. After that they finally left me in peace. But they kept asking me to do street collections for orphans and the poor, which I thought was awful.

I remember one of the collections particularly clearly. It was a very big collection day in winter. The chocolate firm Sarotti – the one with the little Sarotti Moor, a sweet little dwarf in a striped uniform and with a black face – supported the collection. Sarotti chocolate was the best chocolate there was at the time. The company made the uniform available to the Broadcasting Corporation. Someone had said it would be a good thing if the collector showed a bit of imagination and dressed themselves up as fairy-tale characters, and this was in the middle of winter. And then the uniform came to our department, and everyone said, 'Pomseline, you put it on.' And it was the right size for me. It was really made for a small person like me. Out of fabulous fabric. All silk, an expensive, delightful uniform. Great astonishment on the part of the others, so they said, 'You've got to go with your collecting tin to the winter relief collection dressed as the Sarotti Moor.'

And that was what happened. All the famous actors were around, collecting. And people flocked there, just to see the actors, and the politicians and a little Sarotti as well. I was assigned to the Finance Minister of the time. He gave a speech, and I swung the tin and danced around him. And of course I had a huge audience. It was all on Unter den Linden and it also spread to the Tierpark and the Tiergarten. But the main part of it was of course in front of the Stadtschloss and the Reichstag. And I danced around until it was dark, until the collecting was all over and we'd handed over our money, and then we could go home. I remember my mother putting me in the bathtub and trying to get all the brown make-up off me.

Meanwhile Herr Bley had taken up his new job in the Broadcasting Corporation, as head of the board of directors. And I got a lovely room of my own, with another office next to it. It was full of offices, that beautiful, elegant building. It was a sensation at the time – because the building was very modern, with its clinker bricks and its shape.

At first I didn't have much to do. There was a lovely canteen in the building. The other ladies invited me for dinner. There was a wonderful roof garden upstairs, where dinner was served by the canteen staff as well. Working there, I met a few girls with whom I would be friends for a long time, until they all died. Some friendships from my time at the Broadcasting Corporation run through my whole life. One of them is even still alive. She's a year older than me.

Anyway, as quickly as he'd jumped into that job, Wulf Bley was gone. By the end of the year he had said goodbye, I think by Christmas, and then he had left. They couldn't do any-thing with him at the Broadcasting Corporation. He couldn't do anything. He'd just washed up on the tide. He had been a young soldier, a young pilot, and then he'd cheated his way through life, but never did any training or studying. But of course he joined the Party early. I never heard of him again afterwards. He was just one of the old fighters that the Nazis had promised to look after once they were in power. They wanted to put him somewhere or other, but like many others he wasn't what you would call a genius. At any rate, I stayed at the Broadcasting Corporation.

It was thanks to that lucky encounter with Wulf Bley that I had a contract, and a very nice contract too. Oh, I can't remember how much exactly now, but anyway I was making over 200 marks a month. That was crazy money. Compared with what I had got by on for years, it was a princely sum. At first I worked for the board of directors, and then in the office of the former directors. That wasn't terribly honourable in itself, because there were people there who were due to be shunted off – all the secretaries who had been senior in the former Broadcasting Corporation. They had worked for the Jews, because most of the board members had been Jews, who had all been thrown out or sent to the camps; or at any rate out of the broadcasting centre. The secretaries of the Jewish staff members had been sent to the former directors' office to just make copies or duplicates.

Then I had some bad luck and some good luck at the same time. Shortly after starting at the Broadcasting Corporation I fell ill with a protracted cold that went to my lungs. It got worse and worse, and then I was told I should apply to the health insurer for convalescent leave, in order to spend at least four weeks on one of the newly established homes on the Baltic coast. And the doctor actually agreed, and sent me to the island of Föhr [in the North Sea] for a cure. In the end I spent six months in the sanatorium, and the Broadcasting Corporation transferred my money to me every month.

Having that kind of luck was unimaginable at the time. Later I had to go for another cure, but that one lasted for only three months – all paid for by the Broadcasting Corporation.

After that, I switched to the press department of the Broadcasting Corporation and went to the Rundfunk exhibition. They discovered I did brilliant shorthand, so I wrote out the speeches of politicians and others. I even wrote out an early speech by Goebbels when he opened the exhibition. I was really very good and very quick at shorthand, and that was a big bonus for the press department. So I really liked working there.

A little while later I ended up in the Zeitfunkabteilung.[3] Of course I liked that best of all. With my men. All ages, so there were the reporters and football reporters. Eduard Roderich Dietze,[4] he did the tennis commentaries. Rolf Wernicke[5] did football. Professor Holzamer,[6] he was another reporter. Later he was the first person in charge of [the broadcaster] ZDF.

So I had a lot of work at that time. Everything started in the morning with a huge spread of coffee and cakes, and then they discussed things that were happening in Berlin and in the world. Then the radio cars went out – 'Echo-Wagen', they were called – the outside broadcast vehicles with the reporters. We had an Echo in the morning, an Echo at lunchtime and an Echo in the evening. Important visits from foreign dignitaries, princes or football matches, concerts and theatrical performances. There was a lot of stress. You couldn't keep to any mealtimes or meeting times, but in the evening we always ended up having a convivial gathering. Sometimes only with a beer in the canteen, or at Eugen's – a wonderful Berlin local.

Most of the reporters were unmarried, although some were already married, and they went home after work. Somebody always had a car, and that was quite special in those days. But the reporters all had one, so I was always driven home. I was simply one of the guys and had a few wonderful years.

I particularly like to remember the 1936 Olympic Games, and of course the Broadcasting Corporation was involved in those. It was a wonderful time. More than anything it was possible for us to meet foreigners. I remember a friend called me up and said, 'Hey, I met an Indian or a Japanese person yesterday, anyway, someone from a completely different world.' And he had heard that she knew someone in the Corporation, and he really wanted to take a look at the Corporation. And then she approached me to see if I could make that possible. She said, 'I sent him to you – he should be there any minute, so you're prepared.' And he did come. He even spoke German, otherwise I wouldn't have been able to talk to him. And then one of the senior staff members guided him through the building, in so far as he could show it to him. We had arranged to meet the man for dinner that evening. It was a sensation, being with someone who spoke a different language. That was something special. Tell a child that today, a twelve-year-old.

Berlin was in a great state of excitement. Berlin was the most hospitable city in the world. Everyone had been asked to make rooms available, because there weren't enough hotels and bed and breakfasts. Of course we made a room available as well. You got money for it too. Ten marks a night. But it was also a great honour to have a foreign guest. I still remember that the Olympic Games had already begun, and no one had contacted us. My parents had cleared out their bedroom. They'd made it very beautiful. And no one came. But then, on the third or fourth day of the games someone from the Olympic Committee office in Berlin called to ask if we were still taking guests. Yes, of course, whenever you like! And then a couple from Holland came. So there was great excitement, and none of us went to bed. They arrived with tickets that they'd ordered in advance, and were a terribly nice couple. We walked very proudly through the city thinking, 'We've got Olympic guests as well.' They sent us things from Holland afterwards, biscuits and cheese. It was a great experience.

We were very busy at the Corporation at the time, of course, with one broadcast after another from the Olympic stadium or the area around Berlin. I hardly had time to look at the games. I only went once to an athletic event, and once to a dressage competition. It wasn't easy to get tickets, and it was expensive as well.

But the city was transformed. The Kurfürstendamm was suddenly like being in Paris. The people were all cheerful, and the weather was fine. It was the festival that God Almighty had given the Führer. That was what Berlin 1936 was like. And if you walked through the streets you heard English and French, or you saw Indians; I remember that. The first time we saw people with different skins, not exactly Negroes – at least I don't remember any Negroes – but dark people. I only saw one once at the zoo, but Indians, that was something special.

And of course the reports from the games were provided by the Corporation. We had good people, very good people, who made names for themselves later on and also started working on television. Rolf Wernicke was my immediate boss in sport, and was part of Zeitfunk. All the stations were part of the Reichsrundfunkgesellschaft. And every station was responsible for its own location. But they had to decide who they were broadcasting to.

There was no free speech any more. Everything was supervised and listened in on. I don't know if they put people under surveillance before. But as I found out later, Goebbels went through every film script, however short and apparently insignificant. He poked his nose into everything, raised objections and removed actors or demanded different ones, so he always had an influence on the cast. At the Corporation there were clear directives about what you could and couldn't do. You knew how you had to behave. There were already Party loyalists in the individual departments. Not all of them were 'old fighters'; they were people who belonged to the Party, who had performed certain services. Sometimes they were completely clueless, artistically clueless people. But they had a good Party job; they were also SS leaders. No one would have dared resist or stand up to them.

No individual observers needed to show up any more. The people who had the say at the Corporation were all indoctrinated, after all. And from that point more and more anti-Jewishness probably crept in. You weren't aware of it everywhere, but of course you were in the Corporation Literature Department. But not in children's or women's broadcasting. They had recipes and children's songs. Over time you got to know more and more people, and then you knew if somebody was a hardliner or somebody who would be a nice person if he wasn't in the Party.

Anyway. In the first few years, at any rate until the Olympic Games, Germany was wonderful. And there wasn't any persecution of the Jews – everything was still fine. I never personally witnessed a book-burning. But I read about it, things like that were in the papers, but they were too far away for me. I definitely wouldn't have gone. In higher circles they must have thought more about global politics. But we didn't, it was all very remote.

The first turning points became apparent when the Jewish shops disappeared. But there were very few of those where we lived, and all the others had gone. And at that time people giving up their shops was quite normal in any case. A lot of shops closed, even non-Jewish ones. Then gradually, even in our part of town, Jewish shops were boycotted. Even in our very peaceful and in fact completely apolitical Südende. It was a quiet suburb, and half of the people were villa owners anyway. Even so, they'd had dealings with the Jews for a long time. My father always had a Jewish clientele.

I myself had worked for a Jew for four years, and only noticed in the last year that something was happening. He wasn't going to stay. Then we read in the paper that Jews had emigrated. I sometimes thought, he could be one of those. But that always vanished from consciousness again. You didn't immediately connect it with any terrible things, and you couldn't talk to just anyone about it.

I still remember us drifting slowly towards war, but before that, in March 1938, I was on my way to Graz with the reporter

Rolf Wernicke. I was able to talk to him openly. We wanted to have a few cheerful days with friends. He had a radio in the car, and suddenly he stopped and said, 'The time has come!' We drove back to Berlin and had to do a broadcast from there. That was the Anschluss: the annexation of Austria. Wernicke was anything but a Nazi; he wasn't interested in that. He was interested in girls and his football reports. The Anschluss was reported all over the place. Supposedly the whole German people were on their feet; the people in the Corporation made sure of that. Everything was twisted in accordance with the rules thanks to thousands of willing helpers and cheerers-on, none of whom had the faintest idea what was going on. They were all as stupid as I was.

When the concentration camps were set up, the first time we heard 'KZ', meaning 'concentration camp', they said: the only people who get put in those are those who have said something against the government, or who caused fights. Well yes, we thought, of course they're not going to put them in prison straightaway. They were put in a concentration camp to be re-educated. No one gave it a thought. Yet our top announcer in the Rundfunk – Jule Jaenisch, a wonderful man, the whole Rundfunk wouldn't have existed without him – who read the whole news in the morning, at lunchtime, in the evening – Jule Jaenisch was in a camp.[7] 'Yes, but why?' 'They say he's homosexual.' 'Oh for heaven's sake, him – gay?' Homosexual was... homosexual was something terrible in those days. What kind of people were they? And Jule Jaenisch was such a nice, friendly man. 'Yes, yes, they're friendly, but they're homosexual.' We really were a repressed bunch.

Then all of a sudden our Rosa Lehmann Oppenheimer was gone, and her shop was shut. They had to leave. So many Germans were coming from the East at this time. We were told over and over and over again: the Sudeten Germans are all coming home to the Reich, and the villages are empty and must be repopulated. And in go the Jews. They're all together at last. Yes, we believed that. We bought that. And so many foreigners were coming here all of a sudden. They sang differently, they spoke differently, they looked for accommodation here and they lived here, and off went the Jews, whether they wanted to or not. What really happened... They still don't believe us... they all think we knew everything. We knew nothing. It was all kept nice and quiet, and it worked.

There was a little Jewish department store, and my Dr Goldberg was still there, and Papa's customer next door, Herr Levi. They still went in and out. But very slowly... one or another wasn't there any more. But how, what, why? We didn't know. Until that terrible business in November 1938 – the night of the Reich pogrom.

We were all shocked that such a thing could happen. That they should have beaten up Jewish people, people of any kind, and that they had broken the windows of Jewish shops and taken things out. In all parts of the city. Well yes, that's where it really began. We were shaken awake. And then somebody, a friend or relative, said that somewhere neighbours had been taken away by people in uniform. They collected them and drove them away in trucks. Where to? No one knew. Of course that was shocking for everyone who had never paid much attention to politics, and that included us... Terrible.

Of course, I was completely unaware of all of that, apart from reading and the reports on the radio. But a friend of mine, or rather her sister, came crying to us at some party or other and told us that her Jewish boss had been attacked and beaten black and blue. He was only just able to get to his flat, and he was going to leave Germany straight away. Ludwig Lesser[8] was his name. And he did it, too. Some of the ones who said they didn't give a damn – and they just had a valuable wardrobe, or a grand piano or who knows what – they left everything right where it was and they were gone. So the clever ones got out. And then there were the poor, trusting souls who couldn't do anything, and who had supposedly been told they had to leave everything right where it was, and that they would end up in fully furnished flats in Czechoslovakia. And everyone believed it, because that was where the refugees were coming from: 'home to the Reich' was the motto. And I thought: right, for God's sake, perhaps the father used to sit at a desk here, and now he's supposed to be mucking out the byre. But that was what it was. It was a measure taken; we all understood that. We all believed that. We repressed it. Everything calmed down again for a while and we just got on with things.

At that time it wasn't easy to assert yourself professionally as a woman, but once you had, it was acknowledged. But in fact you were supposed to get married and have children – that was the thing worth striving for. In the Rundfunk, we tended to be the intellectuals. Not the dutiful German women with braids around their heads and stout shoes and wide skirts, and of course we rejected all that. We'd heard too much about

America, about jazz, and in that respect we already felt we were a bit special; we were the ones who had a better understanding of the modern age.

There were Nazi women's groups as well. We weren't interested in that. Of course the people I was with knew Jewish writers and sometimes listened to the radio from London. But those were things you could only talk about if you were very, very sure of the person you were talking to. You had to be incredibly careful in those days. You had to be careful not to be denounced.

And then it kicked off. I remember the summer of 1939, and I very clearly remember the day war broke out. I can still see myself standing in the Corporation building, in the office by the door, and hearing over the loudspeakers that German troops had reacted to an attack by Poland in the early hours. I remember that moment as if it was yesterday. And I also remember that everyone was very upset. Everyone. They were all younger people working at the Corporation. There was no cheering, no 'YES!' And no 'Quite right!' Everyone was deeply upset. I remember that very clearly.

And then the first reports of fallen reporters started coming in, including a friend of mine, Otti Kreppke, and a cute young volunteer who fell very quickly, in the first days of the war in the east. One reporter after another was called up. To Poland, then to Russia or Africa. Only a few survived it. And later, when Germany felt at home in Paris, in France, some of the older reporters went to Paris instead of the front. They had a great life. They always brought something very nice back with then: a bottle of cognac or some smart gloves. One of them once brought me back an amazing hat. But the department was getting smaller and smaller.

Then we suddenly had a different director general: the former director general of Cologne, Heinrich Glasmeier[9] – a nice man. But he brought all his people from Cologne with him and filled all the desirable jobs with his people.

So now we were at war. As long as you didn't have someone who'd been called up, you repressed it. For the time being life went on quite normally. Then there were the food cards and clothes vouchers. I still remember my mother saying, 'Oh, my good God: what am I going to give Hilde for bread?' It was all very difficult. That was what we were worried about. We weren't even afraid for my brother's life. He was at war, but he was fine. It was only when the first bombs fell on German soil that you felt it in Germany, on German soil. Suddenly you had that awareness that we might be getting more of this. But we really didn't care too much about it. And then the death notices started appearing in the papers. More and more, afterwards whole pages were filled with the fallen. That made us more thoughtful.

But we had no doubt that we would deal with it all. And we didn't take the other countries that declared war on us all that seriously. We weren't interested in the rest of the West. Of course we didn't understand at the time that freedom was being taken out of our hands. We could only think the way it had been prescribed for us, printed out for us, what the papers wrote, how the radio explained it. There was only one radio station. There was also Deutschlandfunk, but nobody listened to that. It was either only culture or only science;

no one listened. Everyone in the whole of Germany listened to the same Rundfunk. At any rate the masses, the popular masses did, and we were all part of that. And later in the war we heard that an English station was broadcasting in German and was of course against Hitler. You either laughed at it or kept it to yourself, and only talked about it to people who wouldn't give you away.

Working at Rundfunk wasn't as nice as it had been. After the change of director general, everyone in Berlin was from Cologne. All our Berlin reporters were away in the war. Only old Axel Niels – he was seventy – didn't have to go to the front. So more or less everyone had been called up; we could barely keep the business going. We found it bearable until the bombing raids on Berlin began. As long as the bombs were falling on Freiburg or Lübeck we saw it in the press and were very sad, but now that they were starting to fall on Berlin, things became very serious for us. It involved constant fear. And the longer the war lasted, the more it was concentrated on Berlin, on the centre of that whole wicked society.

We lived with it – you can't be afraid all the time and cry and run away. You live with it, and it becomes everyday life. Increasingly those of us left in Berlin were repeatedly rewarded with titbits, extra coffee and other kinds of preferential treatment. They made sure that people stayed calm, particularly in the capital. And they did stay calm too. Who would protest? The people who still had a bit of strength left were mostly in the war. The ones left behind were harmless women, children, sick people, war-wounded – a shabby crew. The longer the war lasted, the more feeble life became. It basically died away, and the days usually ended at six in the evening. There was less and less traffic. You had to keep to so many rules and regulations. We went along with it; it wasn't such a great tragedy.

But in the first years of the war there were big restrictions on what you could eat. Rationed butter and meat. The basic foodstuffs – even semolina or milk – were all rationed. I didn't do too badly, because I got extra food thanks to the lung disease that I'd come through. I got meat ration cards, and they went flying straight out of my hand. I didn't need them; I got extra butter rations and full-cream milk anyway. My mother was glad that I was so rich, because it all found its way into the family home.

It was a bit of an elite. That was why it was very nice working there. Everything was pleasant; I liked it. Nicely dressed people, friendly people. Yes, I was very superficial in those days, very stupid.

Brunhilde Pomsel

'IT WAS A BIT OF AN ELITE': PROMOTION TO THE PROPAGANDA MINISTRY

Only an infectious illness could have prevented me from switching to the Ministry of Propaganda, Brunhilde Pomsel said in the summer of 2013. The switch to Goebbels's ministry in 1942 was an order that Pomsel could not, by her own account, have escaped, at least not without fear of repressive measures. In 1942 the councillor and personal advisor Kurt Frowein was her first supervisor in the Ministry of Propaganda.

Our personnel department was always used by the Ministry of Propaganda as well. One day, they needed a shorthand typist, and I was known at the Corporation for my shorthand. Suddenly and unexpectedly I was told I had to go to Wilhelmstrasse and introduce myself to the assistant head of department, Feige. So I went. He talked to me and asked me what sort of things I could do. And then he said, 'Fine – from Monday your desk will be here at Wilhelmplatz.' So I said, 'I can't do that: I've got so many unfinished things on my desk. I'll have to sort them all out.'

He wasn't interested. I was simply told to be so kind as to take up my position at nine o'clock on Monday. I went home straightaway and got ready as best I could. But since all my friends at the

Corporation were either at war or dead anyway, I was happy to go. Not everyone felt that way. I remember a colleague I worked with on Topics of the Day, who was also transferred to the Ministry of Propaganda. She was in a state of despair because her parents were former Social Democrats. That was how she had been brought up, and it was her own position too – but now she was supposed to go to the Ministry. She was desperate.

But then I rang her up and she said, 'Hey, I've got a wonderful job. I don't have to have anything to do with the Propaganda Ministry at all any more. I just have to go to the houses where Goebbels lives, his private apartment in Berlin or his villa, and I have to put his record collection – which is in complete disarray – in order and put new things in and throw out old ones. It's a very interesting occupation. I sit in the Minister's study, nobody bothers me, and I'm dealing with music.' She was able to stay there for days, and was invited to join Frau Goebbels for meals, but only if Herr Minister wasn't in. Herr Minister didn't want any outsiders in the house. But Frau Goebbels was very nice, my colleague said. She sat with them at the table. That was always terribly nice. And then she was ordered to go to some castle or other. Hitler somehow found out that Goebbels had someone putting his records in order, and he wanted the same thing, so her role extended to the same activities at Herr Hitler's house when he wasn't there. She didn't see him once. She went to the Berghof[1] and did the same thing there and met a lot of people as a result.

Anyway, that evening I organised a Party membership badge from somewhere for the first day. I assumed you would have to wear one of those around the place, but you didn't. On the contrary, they were all dressed very elegantly. I always thought people would be running about in 'climbing jackets' and blue skirts, like the BDM girls or the Nazi Women's League, and I didn't belong to them either. But no. They were quite normal people.

I was all set to be secretary to the future Secretary of State, Dr Naumann,[2] Goebbels's deputy. He was in the SS. He was an admirer of beautiful, tall, blonde women, and turned me down purely on the grounds of my appearance. I was later told he was supposed to have said, 'I'm not having a Jew sitting in my outer office!' I wore black glasses at the time. My hair was a lovely dark brown. I might have looked a little Jewish, if you wanted to see it that way.

And then I was assigned to another man, Kurt Frowein.[3] He was quite a brash young officer who had been brought back from the front because he had a slight injury that needed to heal. I know he exaggerated his injury a little to get away from the eastern front. He was determined to stay in Berlin, and Neumann appointed him personal advisor to Goebbels. He was assiduous in his work – he was quick – but was a very withdrawn person. Over time I realised why he was withdrawn: because he thought the whole outfit was revolting and only stayed there because he wanted to be in Berlin with his family rather than at the front.

I got on very well with Kurt Frowein. He was married – he'd married young – and his wife was expecting a baby. Goebbels looked after the people around him: they were his personal advisors and press advisors, and this Herr Frowein was practically Herr Goebbels's underpants. Wherever Herr

Goebbels was, he was too. When he went to the toilet, he was always nearby. Wherever Goebbels went, Frowein was there; wherever Goebbels went to eat, he was there. When he was at home, on one of his properties or in one of the houses that belonged to him, he was there and slept there too. He was always on duty for three days and three nights without interruption. He was Herr Goebbels's shadow. Then it was the turn of the next advisor, and he could recover.

I had no idea how it all worked. It was only later that I found out he wasn't the only advisor. There were also a lot of other extremely important people. There were lots of departments in the Propaganda Ministry. There were always managers, and lots of deputy managers. The place was swarming with people who had tasks to perform, even if they only stood there and listened. Anyway, there was always a briefing in the morning when Goebbels was in Berlin, and of course Frowein was there too. Then, within two hours, everything had been chewed over. Out of those discussions came tasks for Herr Frowein, which he then had to carry out. Anything he had to do in writing, I did.

Unfortunately I can't remember lots of the details, but a lot of things were kept strictly secret. I couldn't even write any of it down: above all, nothing about the trials against opponents of the Nazi Reich, which later included the White Rose and the 20 July conspirators.[4] There were several things like that. But ordinary life was still going on, and how it was to be organised in the war – all sorts of things like that were discussed. We had to write about it, so there was a lot of work.

But no clues or instances of resistance ever reached the public eye. Not even about the White Rose – only the absolute essentials. Today, I can't remember how those stories were presented at the time. Among ourselves, we felt enormous sympathy because they were so young. They were still students. It was so harsh, executing them straight away. I'm sure nobody wanted that. But it was stupid of them to do things like that. If they'd kept their mouths shut, they'd still be alive today – that was the general opinion.

It was terrible. You had some good friends that you could talk to about things like that, but only very few. You had to be very careful if you touched on those subjects. We would end up saying: what are you supposed to do? You can't do anything. Before you could think: what's going to become of them? they were already dead. Because of a stupid piece of paper, because of a flyer. That was so dreadful, that sentence back then. Certainly, today I can admire that – young people who just believe that the better ones will carry the day. Everybody has to do his bit. And they just did what they could.

I have the very greatest respect for those people. But I know that I would have done anything to keep them away from their scheme, because I would never have had that kind of courage. Assuming I'd belonged to a circle like that... no, I wouldn't have belonged to it. I've never had the courage for things like that. For all the idealism that was also inside me, it never went so far that I would have taken such a burden on board. To that extent what they did was a bit incomprehensible to me.

We were very upset on several occasions during that period when things like that happened. There were a few cases that the world never found out about. All it took was a simple joke about the Führer: people who did that were arrested and executed, I remember that. I was in the Ministry, and it knocked us all sideways. If you knew someone personally then it was particularly devastating.

But with the White Rose, that was different. If I'd ever been religious – which I never was, even though of course we were christened and confirmed – then at moments like that I would have thrown everything away, I would have lost all my faith in the face of all the things that were happening, in the name of this gentleman. As for me, I couldn't make a stand like that. I'm a coward; I couldn't make a stand. I wouldn't dare. I'd say, 'No, I can't do that.' I'm one of the cowards. But I still try to make it clear when people say, 'I'd have known how to escape the Nazi regime.' No! You couldn't. Anyone who did risked his life. The facts prove it. You couldn't say no, and if you did you paid for it with your life, and there were enough examples of that.

Slowly but surely a big change started happening. The longer the war lasted, the fewer journalists came back from the front. We'd picked up on that. And yet you weren't aware of it on a daily basis; you just went on living. You were only able to see the extent of it later on. But we weren't so aware of the meaning, the terrible meaning of that change, like the persecution of the Jews later on. Generally speaking, when you had no access to certain circles, you were barely aware of the persecution of the Jews. With the exception of a few nice neighbours or businessmen that my father worked with I didn't know any Jews anyway.

Only Eva Löwenthal – I was good friends with her, and the family was very poor; they had a terrible time even in all the last years before the persecution of the Jews. Eva could only just keep her head above water. I was at their house once because Eva was ill – she was in bed and I visited her. And all I remember is that there was hardly anything in the room. No furniture, no cupboards: just a table with chairs, very odd. And Eva didn't have a steady job; she scraped a living from the articles that she was able to write, and which were taken from her, only very rarely, by a few journalists, usually from liberal newspapers. They took things from her every now and again, as she was a very good writer of articles on particular subjects. But that might have happened maybe every eight weeks. The family couldn't live on that. Apart from the fact that Eva herself was so selfish and only bought cigarettes with the money and no food for her parents.

Then I heard that Eva had moved away with her parents, to Friedenau – that must have been in the middle of 1942 or thereabouts. I visited them there once, and they were all living in one room. The whole family – mother, father, her older sister, who sold vacuum cleaners door to door. All in one huge Berlin room. There was nothing there but makeshift beds. I thought: oh, my God, how terrible! And Eva told me that they'd been ordered to work for the city, gardening work or something. And she refused to do that, or she just didn't go, and for that reason their support was stopped. They were just allowed to starve.

The family had been hard up before. That was why we'd taken Eva under our wing a bit. We always invited Eva along if we went for a beer. I remember when I was still at the Corporation and she came and visited me. She wasn't very tall, she had reddish hair, very delicate, very slender, but she already had that Jewish nose. But she was very pretty, and she had gorgeous eyes. And sometimes she came to visit me when I was working on the Topics of the Day, in the current affairs section. She had no money. She went on long walks through Berlin; she walked as far as the Masurenallee and said, I'll pay Pomseline a visit. Because she was incredibly funny and quick, my colleagues had a lot of fun with her. And then somebody said, 'Hey, but she's a little Jewess.' 'Yes,' I said, 'there might be something in that.' But she really was a Jewess. I knew her father and mother. You couldn't get more Jewish.

I visited her often, when I'd been sent to the 'Promi'– the Propaganda Ministry. Their flat was so wretched. I actually took cigarettes with me, but I should really have taken bread. Another time I met her in the office, and she wanted to visit me at the Corporation again, but that was no longer possible. I told her I was now working for Goebbels at Wilhelmstrasse, and that it would be better for her not to go. And she said straight away, 'God Almighty, I'm not going there.' She was still free at the time, so that must have been in 1942 as well.[5]

Eva came to our house quite often, and Mama liked to give her some bread because she knew she was a poor girl – but really her reasons were purely human. It didn't occur to anyone that anything was happening that might put her in danger. We went on with our cheerful and carefree life. At first everything was fine. Everyone made a decent living. We weren't as rich as Croesus, but we could afford the occasional treat and were more concerned with ourselves. We didn't immediately think about those poor people. You don't even now, you don't think about the poor Syrians all the time, who have no home and drown in the sea. Who thinks about them all the time? But when you're sitting in front of the television, then you think: that can't be possible, what's happening at the moment. But it is possible. And it will be possible in a hundred years, not just in a hundred years, but as long as this earth exists, it will still be possible. It's part of being human.

It was quite a long time before I lost track of Eva, and you couldn't talk to her about her situation anyway. And why would you have? We didn't talk to her about problems like that. At that time people where we lived weren't yet disappearing. That started quite quickly when it came. I never saw a single transport of the Jews. Supposedly the trucks laden with Jews drove through the streets of Berlin, I wouldn't deny that, but I never saw them, and in any case they didn't drive through Steglitz. It was a little suburb. Vehicles like that didn't pass there. And no Red Front cars drove through before 1933. It just wasn't something that happened in that area of Berlin. There was nothing political there. That was how we lived: on the margins. On the margins of everything that was happening.

Then all of a sudden Eva was gone.[6] And we couldn't do anything about it. She was one of the people who had been taken away. But they'd been taken away to fill the empty farmhouses in the east. And being in the war is worse, we thought. And if she was in a concentration camp she was safe. No one knew what was happening in them. We didn't want to know much; we didn't want to burden ourselves even more unnecessarily. It was enough that we had to do battle with a lot of difficult things, since food supplies were getting worse and worse. Even though we didn't have to worry that much in Berlin, in fact. There were always supplies, not of everything, but we managed. Coffee was rationed; you couldn't have everything you wanted, as you had previously been able to do in the shops. You had to do without a lot of things.

Of course, in those days we only found some things out from the newspapers. People who had left – writers, for example – and we let them go. All the things that happened to the Jews on a mass scale from 1943 onwards I only found out about when I came out of prison myself. Otherwise I never had anything to do with things like that. Even in the Propaganda Ministry I never heard anything about it. Then there was the time when the White Rose was active. We had absolutely no access to the files. Things like that were kept in safes, and we never got near them.

All of our work in the Propaganda Ministry was in principle very strictly regulated and uniform. You sat at the desk and waited for a job to do. A pile of things came together from all over the building, from all the departments. Everything was prepared for public enlightenment and propaganda: the people had to be enlightened about every area, and in every area propaganda had to be made. The economy, art, theatre, opera, film – everything there was in life, even for the simplest pleasures. Every field had an assistant head of department at the top. There was this civil service principle, it was like a mountain. The minister sits at the top, with the messenger boys at the bottom and us secretaries in the middle.

I didn't think our work was important at all; at any rate I didn't enjoy it. It wasn't rewarding work, the sort of work of which you could say when you got home in the evening: 'That was nice, I did that really well.' It wasn't like that. You went along, you sat there, you typed something, you said something on the phone. I'm sure we were aware when Goebbels brought an actor in to read him the riot act, but they did that very skilfully. There were things that simply didn't reach the public. Goebbels and his assistants kept a lot of things to themselves and nothing came out about them, because everything the Corporation broadcast, and every newspaper, was under the total control of the Propaganda Ministry. And there was only one Rundfunk. There wasn't nearly as much reading material as there is today, and everything had to be authorised by the Promi. And everything that came out of the Corporation passed along a single channel; there was no possible way around that. You no longer had any possibility of forming another opinion. The only possibility – and that was forbidden on pain of death – was to listen to foreign radio stations. Of course there were a lot of people who did that anyway, but anyone who got caught could assume that it would cost him his life. I had no connection with anyone who listened to things like that. I knew a few people who were absolutely opposed to the regime, but they were very careful even with me. People were very careful with me as a rule, even if they knew me privately. You couldn't even tell a stupid joke. In comparison with now: I recently saw something, some satirist who had a go at Horst Seehofer, the CSU [Christian Social Union] politician. That would have been completely out of the question in those days. No one would have dared. I remember the satirist Werner Finck[7] making little cracks against the Nazis. People were executed for things like that: they had their heads chopped off.

There weren't very many stars in our office, and if they did show up, they had something to answer for. At that time I sat by the entrance to the ministerial office, with the big glass door and the carpet and the two armchairs. In my mind I can still see someone sitting there: another actor who had made some stupid remark or written something. He was waiting for a discussion with Goebbels. We all walked past him and at least took a look at him, and thought, oh, you poor bastard, you're going to get one hell of a dressing-down today. I can't remember who it was. It was enough for a letter to be intercepted and fall into the hands of the big cheeses, and the one who wrote the letter was executed for it. Those are things you kept finding out about in passing, and never forgot.

We outside-office ladies always knew when the Minister was coming or going. Then he would stand in the room with us, usually with several people or adjutants; someone was always clinging on to him. We got to our feet and stood politely behind our desks. We stood there motionlessly, and then it was 'Heil Hitler', 'Heil Hitler, Herr Minister', and he was gone. He was often travelling or at the Führer's headquarters. On some of his trips he took one of the secretaries with him, in case he needed someone to write things down. For example, I went with him on an express train to Posen. I had to stay on the train, though, while he delivered a speech.

Sometimes there would suddenly be a ring on the door when there were visitors, and an adjutant just shouted, 'Hurry up, we need someone to take notes!' So I picked up my note-pad and pencil. Goebbels was talking with some important people. He quickly dictated something, and I was already out again. He rarely asked the secretaries in to dictate to them. He had discussed most things directly with his assistants, and then they worked on them with the assistant heads or sometimes with lower-ranking people, and it was only then that we worked, chiefly for his assistants.

Goebbels was a good-looking man. He wasn't tall; he was quite short. He would have needed to be bigger if he had really wanted to cut a figure. But he was impeccably turned out; he had lovely suits, the very best fabric. Always slightly tanned. His hands were well looked after, as if someone gave him a manicure every day. So everything about him was above criticism, beyond any objection. He is supposed to have been very charming, and I can certainly believe that. But with us he didn't need to be charming. We were part of the furniture; we were like the desks that stood there, that was all. But there were no smiles or, if there were flowers, no questions about whether someone might have had a birthday, like we know from bosses who sometimes try to ingratiate themselves with the staff. No, there was none of any of that.

I always said, 'Goebbels just sees us as his desks.' I don't mean that he was snooty, but we were sexless as far as he was concerned. He would never have tried – and we weren't all that beautiful – to approach one of us. After all, he was surrounded by all kinds of screen beauties and models and whoever else there was, so he wouldn't really have had to fall back on the office.

Once I sat right next to him in the theatre. The theatre was under Göring's control. Staatstheater, the Opera and so on, Göring was responsible for, and Goebbels had to keep his fingers out of those. But small theatres – the Renaissance-Theater, the Komödie, things like that – they were under Goebbels's control. So on his birthday he invited friends to the theatre, and two of us secretaries were always chosen. One of us sat on his right, the other on his left. But we weren't even driven there with him. He didn't talk to us either; he just sat in the middle. And yet I know that it was an incredible honour to be invited to an occasion like that.

In comparison with the other ladies I was a latecomer to the Promi. There was someone who had been there from the start: Fräulein Krüger, a slightly older, very nice woman. Goebbels already knew her by name, and if something came up, he turned to her. We treated her with great respect too, because she'd been working there the longest. It was extraordinarily pleasant working with everyone in the room, and I was also struck by the lovely furniture, and the beautiful carpets on the floor. In all the offices there were real carpets, things we didn't have at home. I always appreciated that kind of thing.

Where the big names were concerned, there were all kinds of rumours in the Promi, in spite of all the strictness. Goebbels was supposed to have been having an affair with a Czech film diva, Lída Baarová.[8] He was supposed to have really loved her, and I believe that; I can easily imagine that. There were even rumours of divorce. But Hitler never let it happen. Rumours like that were around even then, and you could never tell what was true and what wasn't. But I could easily imagine that it was the truth.

Otherwise people told lots of stories about him. He was said to have affairs. I'm sure there was something in that, but it wasn't all that significant either. If a man has the opportunity, when he's married and has children, he goes with another woman... There was nothing new about that, and no one thought ill of him for it. On the contrary, people made little jokes about it. But when jokes were told about Goebbels it was all in relation to the female sex.

My relationship with the secretaries was always very good, but in comparison with the Corporation it was never especially friendly. There was a certain distance, but they were all helpful and I enjoyed my time there. Otherwise you had nothing else. There was nothing in Berlin. Everything was shut: theatres, concerts, the cinema.

When I was working on a Sunday, sometimes Goebbels would be collected by his children at the end of the day, and then they would walk home. They had an apartment in the city, beside the Brandenburg Gate. Very nice, well-brought-up children. Not children like the ones you see jumping about the place these days; these were very well brought up. They had a nice way of greeting you, of doing these little curtsies. Very well brought up. So we were always delighted when they came. And if you asked them – they were between five and seven or so – any questions: 'Well, aren't you wearing a lovely dress?!' they were delighted. Or if you said, 'Would you like to type on my typewriter?' 'Oh yes!' That was wonderful for them. When you sat them down at the typewriter and put in a sheet of paper and said, 'All right then, now write a letter to Dad. I'm sure you'll do a wonderful job!' I didn't actually have the feeling that Goebbels saw his children as very important, and Frau Goebbels lived outside Berlin with them a lot. She herself didn't try to play a very important part. With her you actually had the feeling that she was doing everything in her capacity as the wife of one of the most senior men. She didn't impose herself. But that was my impression; I thought she was very nice.

But however nice she was, working in the Promi wasn't necessarily felt to be an honour. But, God, I thought, at least you have a job. I mean, we had good incomes at the Corporation. But now suddenly it went up again – they didn't even take anything off for employee insurance. Nothing was taken off. Then when I got my first wage slip I couldn't believe it. It was 170 marks. A good income. None of my friends were making more than 150 or something like that. They all envied me my high wages. As well as a ministry bonus, tax free, of sixty marks; then the ministry office bonus, tax free, another fifty marks. So I had more wages than I'd previously made before tax, in my hand, except it was no use to me because there was nothing to buy. But it was a nice feeling, and sometimes you could actually buy something.

I had a tailor who had some contacts in France. She called me once and said, 'Frau Pomsel, I've got some lovely fabric that would make a sweet dress for you; I'll be at your house this evening.' 'And how much is it?' I asked. And when she told me, I replied, 'Oh, that's far too dear. Oh go on, make it anyway.' I enjoyed that very much. But that had nothing to do with the Promi. And I didn't even ask for it. It was thrown my way. But you could also buy a pound of butter on the black market for 300 marks if you had connections, or a bottle of cognac for fifty. You could do that. There was a branch of the Corporation in Paris, and I was still in regular contact with them. They always brought me something when they came. Either a small present or this or that perfume. So I did very well. It was a bit of an elite. That was why it was very nice working there. Everything was pleasant; I liked it. Nicely dressed people, friendly people. Yes, I was very superficial in those days, very stupid.

But the people who surrounded Goebbels weren't all Nazis by any means. Even Herr Frowein, his personal assistant who I worked for at first, he would make certain remarks. That was a great demonstration of trust. His main reason for working in the Promi was so that he could stay in Berlin, with the family he'd just started. So it was a kind of egoism. He wasn't one of those people who were always walking around with their arm in the air. And he liked me, not least as a colleague, because he'd worked out I wasn't a Nazi whore. But we never talked about it, you just sensed things like that. We got on well. Some other people didn't really take to him: they all rejected him a bit, because in his work he was very brusque and demanding, and everything had to be done very quickly. You had to guess the meaning of half of the things he said. But I managed, and I got on well with him. Sometimes his facial expression spoke volumes about some of the things he had to organise. He was anything but a Nazi.

Then the director of the film department fell out of favour with Goebbels quite badly, and was dethroned, and Herr Frowein took his place. So all of a sudden from being a little Secretary of State he was suddenly the director of the film department and was able to leave his office job in Wilhelmsplatz. Out to Babelsberg, where UFA had their studios. He said to me, 'What do you say – do you want to come with me?' 'Yes,' I said without hesitating. He said: 'I'll see to it.' So he went to his superior – that was Secretary of State Dr Naumann, Goebbels's deputy – and asked for me to be moved with him. 'No,' he said, 'that's absolutely out of the question. Pomsel is staying here. We're not giving her away!' He refused. Frowein took the job, and I stayed, and now I had to report to Dr Naumann, who had turned me down before. I just worked very efficiently. Oh, God, I can't remember why. We were all very efficient. And I was always there.

Dr Naumann was married too and had children, but he wasn't faithful either. We had a secretary in our ministerial outer office that none of us liked, and Naumann always invited her to his house on Sunday. She told us he had another house in Wannsee, and they went out sailing together. I'm sure she went to bed with him. She was good-looking; a tall, slender woman. But we didn't like her, and she was only there for a few weeks.

During that time – this was in 1943 – there was a terrible large-scale attack on Berlin,[9] and our Südende was the centre of it and was completely destroyed. I was alone in the flat when that happened. I'd just come home. I'd been invited out, and I was dressed in French silk accordingly. But no sooner had

I come home than the sirens started wailing. My God, time to go down to the cellar, so I packed my things together. There was a basket with everything in it, I don't know what, but on top there were mountains of stockings – not tights, I don't think they had those yet in those days, but silk stockings, and they always got ladders. I was good at sorting out those ladders. Someone had invented something: it was this little piece of wood, and there was a kind of snapper on the end of it, and you could use that to save stockings. First mine, then my mother's, then for friends, and then friends of friends. Could you, can you – and so on. They always brought me a bar of chocolate if they had one; those were delicacies. So I always had those mountains of stockings lying on top of the basket, and whenever the siren went off I grabbed my handbag and went down to our cellar with it. All the housewives were down there cleaning vegetables or knitting a jumper or just chatting.

So I picked up that basket and went downstairs in my party frock because the sirens were going off, and it was time, because you could already hear some noises. Then a terrible attack began: the first one we'd experienced. Yes, things had come down in some parts of Berlin before. On Bayrischer Platz, and houses had been destroyed there. But never had an attack been so long and so near and so loud, so it was really terrible. No one did anything; we just sat there trembling with fear. Our final hour had come. Suddenly someone came and said, 'Our house is on fire.' We had an air-raid warden; every house did. Someone to make sure that the buckets of water were full on every landing, with rags beside them. Preparations for a rapid response. Ours was a very nice woman of about thirty, whose husband was away at the war. She went upstairs while the rest of us sat in the cellar. Then she came back and said, 'Yes, everything's on fire, and so is our house. But it isn't so bad yet. We may still be able to put it out.' So everyone who could ran to put it out, and so did I. She looked at us all; I can't remember who was in the cellar. Mostly women, of course, but sometimes there were men there as well. She said to me, 'You should stay down here.' She didn't trust me to do it, because you had to leap up four flights of stairs. The air-raid warden took off her watch – a gold watch – and said, 'You should look after my watch.' She gave it to me; she put it in my handbag. So I stayed down below. They all tried to put out the fire up there with buckets and sponges, but it had gone too far. It burned quite slowly, but it was really burning, so they all came back down.

'We can't do it! We have to get out of here!' But how? By now everything was full of smoke, but you could still breathe. 'We have to get out of this cellar!' But all around us was a sea of fire. And then real policemen or firemen or air-raid men came, I can't remember, several men, and they grabbed us all. Anyone who couldn't walk was pulled or dragged into the street.

I was still carting my basket around with me, and eventually I noticed that the handbag was gone. It had been on top, and the food cards were in it. They were the most valuable possession you had. Those cards were really like losing your passport and never getting another one. Without the cards you got nothing to eat; it was terrible. I remember that we ended up in some strange cellar, where I even went to sleep. And when dawn broke, loudspeakers rang out in the streets. All the residents of those streets were to gather in the city park in Steglitz. It seemed to be all right, so we wandered over there. First of all the Red Cross distributed soup to everyone. But my most important things, my money and everything else, were simply gone. Oh, I was the poorest person in the world. And where was I to go now? My friends had been bombed out as well. No one thought of anyone else, everyone just thought of themselves.

I have to go to the office, I thought. At least there are people there that I know. I've got to go to the office. Of course no transport was running. Traffic was totally paralysed. So I walked.

And then all of a sudden I was standing in our office. They had no idea. Everyone knew that Steglitz had been hit. Steglitz, Südende, Lankwitz. Because I was late, they'd already said to each other, 'I hope nothing has happened — she lives in Steglitz.' But suddenly I was standing there, in that lift. At first they couldn't help laughing when they saw me in my party frock and carrying that basket, until they all worked out what had happened.

Then it was quite touching. Everyone wanted to do something for me; they were kind and pleasant. Then something else happened that I like to remember: when I was standing there bombed out like a poor little thing, suddenly Frau Goebbels's secretary came in. She also had a desk in the ministerial office. But we never saw her and barely knew her. And afterwards she had probably gone to see Frau Goebbels and said she'd seen a victim of that bombing raid and told her about that poor girl there: her colleague standing in the office in her party dress. 'So, hasn't she got anything else to wear?' And then she says, 'Where would she have got anything? It happened last night.' Frau Goebbels would have gone to her wardrobe and said, 'So, can I help her with anything?' She took out a blue suit and said, 'Do you think she could wear that?' The secretary said, 'She's such a tiny little thing; she won't fit into anything. You can't just put a dress on like that.' Frau Goebbels said, 'This suit, maybe something like this will fit her. Or perhaps it can be altered a little.'

Anyway the secretary brought me that suit, and I went to a tailor and two days later I was perfectly dressed. I had never had a suit like that in my whole life. It was a wonderful blue woollen fabric. Lined with white silk. Wonderful. I wore it a lot later on. As the jacket fitted very well, only the skirt had to be shortened. My mother even dragged that suit through the war, and I was photographed in the suit again when I came out of prison. The jacket still fitted. It survived a few things – and even outlived its former owner.

We were the first to be bombed out, and in 1943 things really got going. I often had to stay at work until eight in the evening. And the sirens went off at seven o'clock, so that you couldn't go into the street. The all-clear often didn't come until ten or twelve o'clock, which meant I couldn't get home. We had lovely comfortable armchairs, so I pushed two of them together and had a snooze. We did that often. We had no choice.

When a raid came, we often had to lock up Goebbels's little private apartment. He had a sweet little apartment in the Propaganda Ministry, separate from the ordinary Public Enlightenment and Propaganda business. But access to that apartment was opened up when the air raids increased, because the moment the sirens went off, anyone still at work had to secure everything. It was an old building. So we had to open all the windows, then draw down the blackout blinds. We had these special blinds that didn't let a ray of light outside. Then we had to run water into all the basins and tubs so that we had water to put out the fires. We had to do the same in that little apartment. It was a very nicely furnished flat with lovely carpets, a little kitchen, a pretty little sitting room with very elegant furniture and a bathroom with an enormous bathtub. We had to fill the tub and seal up the windows, and when the alarm was over it all had to be removed again. We sometimes even dared to sit down on the chairs. They had this French pattern – wonderful upholstery. Unbelievably chic. That was where Herr Goebbels's love scenes were supposed to have been played out when he was associating with that Czech actress, Lída Baarová. I saw a film about her later, after the war, when she talked about her love life with Goebbels. I think she probably really loved him very much. I could also imagine that there were moments when he thought: dear Christ, all this political shit! Living with this beautiful woman is much nicer.

The atmosphere in the Propaganda Ministry was the same as in the whole country, but it would soon worsen. Things went into decline, especially supplies, and everything got very much worse. Stalingrad[10] had changed everything – the loss of the army. We sensed that in the Ministry too… For the first months it was wonderful there and after my initial doubts I liked it very much. All the coming and going, the beautiful furniture, the nice people. But then everything collapsed. The whole atmosphere had changed. Stalingrad was played down; they tried to present it as a mere trifle. But they didn't succeed.

Then the war really got going. From then on Goebbels was in the Promi a lot, limping through his office. He couldn't hide the limp. That was a time when you couldn't do as much as you can now. Today they would sort it out in some way so that you didn't notice it. But it was impossible to ignore. He limped in, and his suit could be as smart as you like, and as well fitting, but he limped, and that made you feel a bit sorry for him. He made up for it all with incredible arrogance and self-confidence. Before – he was often shown in early pictures when he was canvassing for Hitler with other people on trucks and things, with a cap – he looked dreadful. Now, he was always a gentleman when he came into the office. Because sometimes there were people with him – you can imagine, they had some pretty tough discussions. Once I remember us all saying, 'He really shouted today,' when he had shouted at somebody or other. We all thought that was incredible. Never again. Just that one time. He was a man who had – what do they say? – composure, self-control.

There were also comical moments. Someone had thought of sending Goebbels's dog to him in Venice. Goebbels had gone to the Venice Biennale with his wife and stayed there for a few days. Someone had probably got word that Goebbels had said it would be nice if his dog were there too, so some eager staff member called us to say that Herr Minister wanted to have his dog in Venice. We said, 'Are they mad, sending a dog on a plane to the Biennale in Venice? As if they have nothing else to worry about, in the middle of the war...' So we thought it was infuriating. Someone was given the task of going to Tempelhof airport and ensuring that the dog would fly to Venice – but accompanied by somebody, with the dog as hand luggage. Some chief of press was flying to Venice every day anyway, taking the latest foreign news so that Herr Minister could keep up to date. That was Herr von Schirmeister,[11] another assistant. Schirmeister was told, 'If you fly tomorrow, take the dog with you to Goebbels. Herr Minister would like to have his dog there.' 'Never,' Schirmeister said. 'I will never do anything like that.' He was a slightly older, sensitive gentleman, who thought this was an infuriating presumption.

It was no good: they handed the poor chap the dog at the airport and he flew with the dog to Venice, but there he was received with the greatest displeasure. I think Goebbels himself was furious. What idiot had come up with the idea of flying that oversensitive, nervous animal all the way there? He was a shy animal, in fact; he was big and beautiful, but if you took a step towards him he always flinched. He had been spoilt, somehow. So the dog was sent back, and that was all in the third year of the war. So there was an almighty to-do from Goebbels. We thought that was a wonderful story; we laughed our heads off.

I discovered his true nature only very slowly. I remember the famous event at the Sportpalast – 'Do you want total war?'[12] We knew Goebbels was delivering a speech that afternoon. At that time all events had been moved to the afternoon, because the sirens went off every evening at half-past six, whether planes came or not. They almost always did; it was very rarely a false alarm. There were no evening events any more, there were no theatre performances, no films in the cinema, everything was moved to the afternoon. So Herr Goebbels was to give a speech in the Sportpalast, and suddenly they were saying that two ladies from the outer office were to come to the Sportpalast too. 'Why?' 'I don't know, they just want two to come.' 'Who?' We all looked at each other, and no one volunteered. Frau Krüger was the oldest so she didn't need to, and it fell to me and a young girl.

An SS man came and put us in an elegant Mercedes. That was a lovely start, and he drove us to the Sportpalast. It was on Potsdamer Strasse, and he took us to one of the rows of seats. Really good seats, very near the speaker's podium. The hall was already full of workers who had been drummed up. For these events, if people in the factories were called on – who wants to go? – at first everyone ducked out. At around this time, certainly. No one volunteered; they were mostly chosen. So they were dragged out of the plants and factories to take part in this announcement in the Sportpalast. I still remember the actor Heinrich George, the father of Götz George, sitting in the third row at the front.

And as soon as we were there, it got going. Frau Goebbels was sitting behind us with two children, and SS men sat next to us; we really were in an elite position, I would say. The marching bands came in, with the usual military marching music and singing and everything else that went with it. Then

Goebbels got up to make his speech. He spoke very well; he was a persuasive speaker. That day he actually became so intense, it was really an outburst – like an outburst in a mental hospital, I would say. It was if he'd said: now you can all do whatever you want. And then, as if every individual in that crowd had been stung by a wasp, all of a sudden they all let themselves go, shouting and stamping and wishing they could tear their arms out. The noise was unbearable.

My colleague sat there with her hands clenched; we were both so horrified by what was happening. Not by Goebbels, not just by the people – but by the fact that it was even possible. The two of us weren't part of this crowd. We were onlookers; we were perhaps the only onlookers.

It came to the point where I don't think even Goebbels knew what he was saying. I lack the words to describe how he managed to get these hundreds of people to the point where no one was sitting down, but they were all jumping to their feet and shouting and cheering. He did it; I don't think even he knew how. I still remember how we stood there, firmly clutching each other's hands, my little colleague and I. It was as if we were frozen to the spot by everything that was happening. Behind us stood an SS man, and he patted us on the shoulders and said, 'At least clap along.' So of course we clapped along. You had to, of course. He even said so. You couldn't exclude yourself; there was no option. We clapped along. It was as if we were drunk. We both had a sense of something very terrible happening.

And then it was over, after they had cheered themselves out. I think that anyone who hadn't cheered along would have been murdered by his neighbours. I don't know. In my whole life I had never experienced anything like that; it wasn't enthusiasm, it was as if they didn't know what they were doing. *'Do you want total war?' 'Yes!'* The 'Yes' was quite unambiguous. The SS man who had brought us drove us home again, and we were both completely horrified by the whole performance. We hadn't grasped what he had been talking about. There was the impression of this clamouring crowd that had no idea why it was clamouring. It was a natural event; the whole crowd could do nothing about it. Goebbels himself probably couldn't either. It seemed to me that he himself didn't understand what he had started. Like a little flame that didn't know what its possibilities were, and then that clamouring crowd. Oh God, they could just as easily have charged forward and killed him.

Until then we hadn't known that side of Goebbels. We had never gone to any rallies of any kind. So we were quite shaken; it was a complete change. But we probably didn't think much more about it than that. We were bowled over by the moment, then we somehow came to terms with it. God, we were young, and we didn't think about it so much, not the way we thought about it later, when it was all too late. You weren't even aware of it yourself. While now, when so many years have passed and so much has happened, I see it all quite differently. Much more deeply, and much stranger. That one person was capable of putting hundreds of people in a state where they were shouting, shouting, shouting: 'Yes, we want total war!' If you tell somebody that today, they would just shake their head and say, 'Right – were they all drunk or what? What was it that made those people shout like that?' But they had to. They had really been put under a spell by a single person.

I mean, there are psychologists and science that deal with that whole thing, about how a thing like that is possible. When I remember that again, I think: how was that possible? That it had such an effect on us? They didn't shout because they had to shout, because somebody had said to them, 'Now go to the rally and then you all have to shout.' No, they shouted at that moment because at the front someone was telling them something they agreed with. Like Jesus did or... I don't know. There are things that explain why people en masse do inexplicable things. If they were asked about it, they themselves would be startled.

All I can say about Goebbels is that he was an outstanding actor. He was a good actor. Hardly any actor could have given a better performance of the transformation of a well-brought-up, serious person into a crazed brawler than he did; you can certainly say that. He was unrecognisable. That was another thing that left us so shaken by that Sportpalast event. A person you see almost every day in the office – nicely turned out, elegant, almost a noble elegance – and then that raging dwarf. You can hardly imagine a greater contrast.

At that moment I found him terrible. Frightening. But then I repressed it again. I never lionised him or anything like that. Not even later, when he came into the office and asked us politely for something. I already had in the back of my head how he had shouted in the Sportpalast: and here you are now playing the part of the elegantly dressed civilian.

A short time later there was an invitation to dinner from Goebbels. The minister had been informed that the ladies in his office sometimes had to spend the night there, because there were no available means of transport after the air raids. A gesture was required. So they said that at some point the minister would invite the secretaries to dinner, but not all at once. Always two at a time, to a personal dinner.

Two of the secretaries got the ball rolling and the next day came enthusiastically into the office and told the others: 'We were collected from the office, in a car, of course, and brought to Schwanenwerder, and there was Frau Goebbels, and there was fabulous food!' No exaggeration – there was a war on, after all. Goebbels always set a good example: he didn't put on anything too luxurious. But everything was lovely and pleasant. 'It was a terribly nice evening, you can look forward to it when your time comes,' they said.

It was a few weeks before it was my turn, and I looked forward to it very much. It started exactly like this: a limousine pulled up, and an SS man took us to Wannsee, Schwanenwerder. We went in, and we were led into the dining room. There was a big table laid out, and at least twenty people standing around – Gauleiters or Deputy Gauleiters – and I knew some of them from visits or because we'd even dealt with them before. So we weren't alone with Herr Goebbels. Then Goebbels came and greeted us with a handshake, and we sat down. I sat beside him, on his right side; I felt very honoured.

Then we ate. But he didn't say anything to me – he just talked about unimportant matters. The food was nice; I think there was a goose, which in itself was cheering. Then Goebbels sounded off across the table. Sometimes someone else spoke as well, but Herr Minister was the main speaker. He ate quite quickly and not very much, and so did the others. I had been told beforehand: 'Don't put off eating for very long. When Goebbels puts his fork or his knife down, then you stop eating and you don't eat any more. So you have to eat what you're served very quickly, so that you get the benefit of it.' I followed that advice.

The dinner was over, and then there was pudding. Politics and air raids were the main topics. He only exchanged banalities with me and never asked any personal questions. How long have you been here? Or: are you married? Do you have relatives, maybe you have a husband or a father who's at the war? Nothing. He didn't ask me a single personal question. And Frau Goebbels wasn't there at all, which was the big flaw in the evening, because she would have turned it into something jolly and cheerful, with a lot of charm. That was missing from the evening. Unfortunately, I had got the wrong day.

Then we were led into a side room, and there was this sort of screen there, showing some stupid film that had just come out. We were allowed to watch that, and then we were served something else, a mocha or something. And then the SS man reappeared and drove us back to the city. My colleague and I were very disappointed by that evening.

After my release from prison I was often asked what kind of things crossed our desks. As administrators, we also had to deal with very harmless things. There wasn't really that much work to do. We sat there in the outer office, and we made lots of phone calls. All very simple things, the kind that happen in any firm where not everyone knows straight away what's going on.

No one at the Corporation ever told me, for example, what they were able to listen in on via that London station. They must have had critical things to say. I didn't have friends like that. Perhaps people were a bit cautious with me because I was sitting in Goebbels's office, so they didn't want to tell me anything.

But we didn't want to know anyway. We knew it was a terrible war that was served up to us as a necessary war, a war we needed to preserve Germany, which was treated with hostility by the rest of the world. We had no friends abroad either: our friendships and acquaintances weren't as extensive as that. We were very much limited to ourselves, and even more so as a result of the war.

As far as we outer-office ladies were concerned, our function was simply to be ready to leap in. We were a cheerful, harmonious gang. We worked well together. We were a nice collection of colleagues, nothing more than that. Our desks were in a rectangle. All the reports, requests and changes produced in the building landed on our desks, but lots of things, probably including the most controversial, had been decided already. Only things that were particularly important reached all the way up to the Minister himself, and we got those on our desks. I remember that we weren't allowed to scribble on them. We always had to use blue ink. Not red, not green. Green was the Minister, I think; red was the Secretary of State. I can't remember if those colours are right. But anyway the colours indicated who the documents were meant for.

There are lots of things I can't remember sixty years later. The phone was constantly ringing, but not for Goebbels. He didn't get phone calls directly from his people, from his fellow ministers. He had the latest invention from Siemens: a telephone table, so that you didn't have to dial, you just typed, then you got straight through to Hermann Göring. But those connections were closed to us. We could press the keys as much as we wanted, but nothing happened. Otherwise we could have called anyone at all – very important people.

Of course, much of the work involved embellishing the bare facts from the front or in the Reich; they were corrected on instruction to make things look more positive for us. That was the fundamental principle of Public Enlightenment: the people were now enlightened, when they had previously always been lied to by the other governments. That had been the fundamental principle of the Nazis, but I can't remember any examples today.

Otherwise our days were always exactly the same. Really controversial things like the Scholl case [the White Rose] didn't cross our desks. But Herr Frowein, Goebbels's personal advisor, handed me all the files, the court files, unsealed. I was to put them in a safe. 'Please don't look inside,' he said. And I didn't, because my boss asked me not to. Or maybe he said: 'I'm relying on you not to peek.' It was all very quick, and then he went away. I was left alone with the thing and didn't look inside. And I thought, oh, God, I'd love to. But I won't: he's relying on me not to do it, so I won't do it. I was still very proud because of the trust he put in me. That was more important than satisfying my curiosity. I thought that was very noble of me; I'll never forget that.

Towards the end of the war we kept getting these coloured sheets of paper, pink or yellow. They contained the latest truths, not least about figures – casualty numbers in battles, and about rapes of German women by the approaching Russians. Unimaginable. We passed that on to the Corporation and the newspapers. If it said 'Twenty women were raped in the village' we turned it into thirty and so on. Those things were conveyed to the people in an exaggerated version. The terrible crimes of the enemy were all multiplied. I remember that very clearly.

The truly important things, and some secret orders, were always stored in safes. Only the advisors had keys to those. There were lots of things that I couldn't have looked at on the way to the safe, given that it was only a few steps away. The whole thing took only a couple of minutes. I can only vaguely remember which files I held in my hand – lots from the People's Court. I didn't write a word about them myself, or take any dictation about them, and neither did the other ladies. No one knew anything. And we were under obligation, I had to take an oath.[13] When I joined I'd been given a book about the rules of behaviour and also about correct practices. For example, that you couldn't work with a red pen or a green one. Strictly forbidden. You had to know all sorts of things like that. I had to study everything; it was all very strict. It was the only thing we knew. Sometimes we found out when a famous writer had written a letter with a disparaging remark about Hitler or Goebbels. He was arrested and executed straight away. You knew about things like that.

Goebbels also wrote his speeches himself and only dictated them to Richard Otte,[14] a very nice man – he took shorthand, and was constantly following him around. Goebbels dictated everything to him. A huge article by Goebbels appeared every Sunday. It was just as new to us when it came out on Sunday as it was to everybody else. Otte recorded it: he had a special office, and of course a secretary. Goebbels dictated it, then it was sent to the *Völkischer Beobachter* – that was the main newspaper – and they published it. But we had nothing to do with that either. As I say, we were highly paid shorthand typists and secretaries, who could also relax from time to time. But we always had to be there, on the dot. And that time when I was bombed out, people were very generous. You had to run around to an awful lot of offices – to do this and that. I was very generously allowed to do all that.

One day something really happened – and to my regret I wasn't there, because it was my day off. We had days off now and again. I spent mine in Neu-Babelsberg [near Potsdam], where a colleague of mine lived. At about midday I suddenly heard something about the attempt on Hitler's life on the radio. I rang the office straight away – the Promi – and said, 'What's going on?' 'For God's sake, just be glad you didn't come into the office today! We have no idea what's going on. We're just looking out of the window. The whole of Wilhelmplatz is full of soldiers, with rifles. It's not a parade, they're ready to shoot. There's supposed to have been an attempt on the Führer's life. We're all surrounded; no one's allowed to leave the building. We have no idea – we know nothing, and Minister Goebbels isn't here either. We have no idea how we're going to get home; we can't leave.' They were totally desperate.

Now I had my ear pressed to the radio, and there were constant reports about it, about everything that was happening. It turned out very quickly that Hitler was still alive. In the Promi they were just scared for their lives when they saw they were surrounded. I was very unhappy not to be there when something was happening. I wasn't glad to be in Potsdam. And then all I know is what everyone knew. The whole story; I found out all about it. And those discussions with the officers in the People's Court. It's all well known. So I just know all of that as an onlooker.

We found out other things from day to day. I know that actors sometimes visited Goebbels. But we didn't find out what happened between them. It was about that one film, *Jud Süss*.[15] There were some films about the historical Jewish question. About 200 years ago. Ferdinand Marian[16] was a very good actor. He had to play that Jew. He played him wonderfully well, and the whole film was great. But he hadn't wanted to play him; he was forced. They probably said, 'If you don't play the part you'll end up in a camp.' He resisted, but he had to do it. The film was a great success, but I'm sure he wasn't proud of it.

Goebbels was involved in every film that promised to be a great success. Not in every film, but films that were promising had to be shown to him first, and he himself had to make corrections to the cast. I know that. I didn't see it, but you knew. That was his relaxation, his plaything; he probably needed that to counteract all the unpleasant jobs he had to do. He enjoyed that, and he wouldn't let anyone take it away from him.

I remember the last big film[17] that Goebbels was involved with. It was already coming to an end. It was deliberately staged in such a way that the people would bear witness to the unconditional will to victory. That was the plan, and in the weekly newsreels we were always the victors, of course. He re-edited that one furiously. He got very involved in everything, even art. Art, particularly Teutonic art, was fostered a lot even in school. Particularly the heroic sagas from the old days. There were also a lot of Austrian films. I can still see many of them in my mind's eye. I even got to meet actors like Attila Hörbiger, and Heinrich George, the father of Götz George – he was a great actor. But a lot of Jewish actors got away in time and went to America. We had previously had some good Jewish actors at UFA.[18] Good people who all got away in time.

I didn't always have the money, particularly when the first films were on, before I started at the Corporation. But in those days that was the chief entertainment, because theatre was more expensive, and the opera was quite out of the question. In wartime, of course, culture was very restricted, because first of all you had to eat. In the meantime there was radio as well – radio was an important form of entertainment too, of course. By now there was only the Reichsender Berlin; especially in the evening, at about eleven o'clock. Broadcasts came from the exclusive hotels – Adlon, Excelsior, Kaiserhof and Bristol Unter den Linden. There were really good hotels and bars, and the bar music was broadcast by the Corporation, with the latest popular songs. I spent nights on our chaise-longue when everyone was in bed and asleep. I knew all the songs, I could sing along with everything. Oh, it was wonderful! Sometimes Mama found me when I'd gone to sleep like that. That was lovely. That was all the culture we had!

I felt a bit as if I had died inside. I'd often been frightened in my life before. But now I was icy cold — unfeeling. I'm trying to say: all my feelings were gone. There wasn't even any room for fear. Just this feeling: it's all over. Nothing more than that. Over. It's all over.

Brunhilde Pomsel

'LOYAL TO THE END': THE LAST DAYS IN THE PROPAGANDA MINISTRY

Shortly before the downfall, Brunhilde Pomsel made a serious decision that forced her to stay in the air-raid shelter of the Propaganda Ministry next to the Führer's bunker containing the last faithful followers. She only found out in dribs and drabs what was happening in the bunker from the last members of Hitler's retinue, who included Hans Fritzsche,[1] one of the senior officials in Goebbels's Ministry and a well-known radio commentator, and Goebbels's adjutant Günther Schwägermann,[2] who burned the bodies of Magda and Joseph Goebbels at the end. After Goebbels had refused to surrender, Hans Fritzsche decided to offer to surrender in his own right. Before Fritzsche crossed over to the Soviet side with two of his officials, Brunhilde prepared the white flag for the surrender. After brief negotiations Fritzsche is supposed to have announced, on behalf of the German government, that the Soviet side had accepted the surrender. On the evening of 1 May 1945, General Helmuth Weidling, Commander in the Battle of Berlin, ordered his troops to abandon fighting.

I still remember our air-raid shelter in the Propaganda Ministry, when Dr Naumann was over with the Führer, in the Führer's bunker. I have a dim memory of an iron plate or something somewhere. That was very much at the end of the war, when they were already flying over the cities in broad daylight. There was a morning raid over Berlin – not a large raid, but they flew so that you could see the planes, and they were enemy planes. Dr Naumann sat at his desk and dictated, and I wrote, but I was so frightened I couldn't keep writing. He laughed his head off, and said, 'Good God, I'll tell you when things get dangerous!'

At last he stood up, quite calmly, and said, 'Now come with me.' And then he walked with me across the square to the door. I remember the planes were no longer in the sky; I think by then they had gone. Suddenly I saw that there was a flight of steps leading down. He left me on my own, shook hands with one of the SS men, then led me back to the Ministry. I'd never seen that before. And later, when I was among the people again, I heard about it. The Führer had a bunker under Wilhelmsplatz. I'd never heard of it before.

I was very scared during the war, I remember that, when there were air raids, and some women, mostly hysterical women, said, 'Oh, if only a bomb would hit us and everything would be over!' Then I could shout, 'No, no, we need to live! I want to live! I don't want to be killed by a bomb!' I had an incredible will to live. I have no idea what for. I wanted to stay alive. I didn't want to be killed by the war.

At the end of the war we spent almost all our time sitting in that horrible cellar in the Propaganda Ministry, still believing in that stupid Wenck Army,[3] which would move round the back of the invading Russians and attack them from behind, and then the decision would have been made and the war won for us. When we went into the cellar, in April, a day after Hitler's birthday,[4] I still believed in it. By then no one talked to anyone any more. But we believed all of that and felt safe. We were informed about some of the things that went on in the Führer's bunker; someone always appeared to tell us what was happening. Once Herr Naumann came, I remember that. He was checking to see if we had anything to eat. I remember eating asparagus by the pound in those days. Raw, out of tins, tinned asparagus. Someone else often came, but I can't remember his name any more. Goebbels's adjutant, Herr Schwägermann, appeared one day – Günther Schwägermann, a fine man, a nice man – and he delivered a bit of a report.

He told us that Goebbels was with his family in the Führer's bunker. And the children? The children too, the whole family, they're living in the bunker now. Well, now we had a clearer idea. The nice flat near the Brandenburg Gate was too dangerous, and the Russians were no longer just bombing from the air: they were already firing rocket launchers. That was why he had taken his family to the bunker.

In our first few days in the bunker a telephone was still working. I remember that we phoned Hamburg – you could still do that from Berlin. Afterwards it all went dead! We just sat there and looked around the cellar to see what we could find. There was plenty of wine, but we needed something to eat as well. We found preserves, and we ate those. You couldn't go outside and fetch something back; you couldn't stick your head out of the shelter at all.

Then people who had been wounded by the Russians in street battles were brought to us in the cellar. So there was just a very small gang of us waiting. We were slowly coming to understand that the thing about the Wenck Army, which was supposed to come and liberate us, was probably not quite correct. We had two large rooms, some of which were equipped with camp beds. Someone could sleep on one of those for four hours, then he would have to get up and make room for someone else. It went on like that for a good week. We were always aware when orderlies came to the building and brought in more patients. There were noises of some kind, so we closed the doors and locked ourselves away a little. What else were we supposed to do?

Oh, God. We vegetated! We knew that something had to happen. Every now and again someone came over from the Führer's bunker, because Naumann was over there, and the SS soldiers kept us up to date with what was going on. So there I was in the cellar, and then Schwägermann came in and said, 'Hitler's taken his own life.' For the first time we were all exposed, standing there. No one said anything; everyone had their own thoughts on the matter – and then he disappeared again. He only wanted to tell us because he knew we had no idea what was going on in the Führer's bunker. That was the first thing we learned. Everyone knew what it meant: the war was over and lost. The war was over. That was clear to all of us.

I can't remember how we found out the details; I think there was a whole day and a whole night in between. In my memory there's a long time in between, at least a day and a night. Then Schwägermann came again and said, 'Goebbels has taken his own life. And his wife too.' 'And the children?' 'The children too!' After that there was nothing more we could say.

Oh, God, that certainly wasn't nice. We probably tried to make sure that the alcohol didn't run out. We needed it urgently. Maybe not everyone, but certainly people were 'tippling' a lot there. You had to numb yourself. We had no work to do. And the mood? There was fear, but there was also a sense of not being able to change anything. There was also a certain apathy. Now the time had come. We didn't know what had come exactly – but it was all over. I didn't even think: will they shoot me now, or will the Russians rape me? None of that mattered. I felt a bit as if I had died inside. I'd often been frightened in my life before. But now I was icy cold – unfeeling. I'm trying to say: all my feelings were gone. There wasn't even any room for fear. Just this feeling: it's all over. Nothing more than that. Over. It's all over.

There's one other thing I remember about the previous few days. It was the last day when we still had our typewriters on the terrace at the Goebbels house. Dr Collatz[5] came – another of Dr Goebbels's personal advisors, a very nice man – and he said, 'Pomseline, my wife and daughter are still in Potsdam and I want to say goodbye to them before things get any worse here. I've organised a motorbike.' There was a transport department, part of the Ministry, and there were motorbikes as well. You weren't allowed to ride them by then, and you couldn't, because there was no petrol, but Dr Collatz had managed to borrow a motorbike with petrol for his journey to Potsdam. And then he said, 'I remember you told me your parents were now in a house in Potsdam.' Because our flat was uninhabitable again: everything was broken – all the windows, all the doors – because of bombs that had fallen nearby. 'I can take you along,' he said. 'I'm setting off tomorrow morning and then coming back. We can do a quick trip.' 'Yes,' I said, 'I'd love to come with you to see my parents again.' With me on the pillion, he drove me there, said goodbye, and said, 'I'll come back at seven in the evening and collect you again.'

I spent the whole afternoon with my parents. Lunchtime and afternoon. Then it was seven o'clock, and Dr Collatz didn't come, then it was eight, then nine. I had no idea how to contact him. Of course my parents were still awake as well. But then eventually Mama said, 'It's time to go to bed.' We woke up at seven the next morning – Dr Collatz hadn't come. Now I was very agitated, because in those days there were lots of people who suddenly didn't turn up for work. Who didn't care about anything, and who were suddenly gone. There were lots of people who got wind of what was coming and fled. But I had a job to do and I was part of the team. I had to go into the city; I had to, I had to go back.

My mother said, 'So, must you really?' – 'Yes, I must!' I was very dutiful; I was extremely important. I went to the station, which was ridiculous. There were no actual rail connections any more. But in fact a train did come: a local train heading for Friedrichstrasse station. I don't know why it came! It stopped and picked me up. There were other people in it. Essentially, during those days, everything had collapsed. I went from Friedrichstrasse station straight to the Propaganda Ministry and into the cellar, and then I was in there for about another ten or eleven days.

Somebody later told me what had happened to Dr Collatz. He went to see his wife. He had a little daughter of about ten or eleven: a disabled child, but her parents were very attached to her. She was their only child. He rode there, took them both to the Wannsee, and shot his wife and child and himself. He extinguished all three lives. So he had never planned to come back, but neither could he tell me what he had planned, and he couldn't say to me that he wasn't coming back. He went there with very firm intentions and did it deliberately, because he thought he had no more prospects in his life.

Did Dr Collatz want to save my life? Certainly. He must have thought, 'If she's worked it out somehow, she will use the opportunity to stay in the country.' In retrospect that was enormously stupid of me. It really was a time when you knew that the war couldn't be won. Why did I have to go back? It was stupid of me. But I hadn't thought about what would happen next. I think by that point I couldn't feel anything: it was as if I was dead, pale and extinguished. It's hard for me to talk about things in the past and what state of mind I was in.

Now of course I'm glad that I always coped with things well. It could have been quite different, but then I wouldn't have had the chance to think about it, and it would all have been over for me as well. Today I think that for all the things that happened to me, I mean things that weren't good – particularly bad things – well, I dealt with them reasonably well. I'm glad about that, and I'm also content with myself. And I have every reason to be.

Everything was nice so much of the time. In between times I was very, very happy. It was never actually completely boring. But sometimes it was a bit boring. My God, a life like that can't just consist of highs and lows. There were long periods of resting in between. I had those, but so does everybody. There was no miracle weapon and no Wenck Army to come and save us. We stopped thinking, full stop. We put our hands in our laps and thought, 'How's it going to end?' There were a few real idiots – I was one of them – who thought the Wenck Army, the one that was going to attack the Russians from behind, would make it, and that would be the climax of the war. Now the Wenck Army is killing the Russian soldiers, and we've come up smiling. There weren't very many of us in the hard core of the Propaganda Ministry. I didn't believe it by pure faith; I just thought there was no other possibility, just that one. The army exists, it will come and make a clean sweep and then everything will be fine.

The Wenck Army wandered through our brains like ghosts until the very last days. Eventually we all worked out that the wool had been pulled over our eyes. Some people worked it out a bit earlier than that. I was so stupid: I went on believing it practically until the last day. Because I really couldn't imagine anything else. We couldn't lose the war, after all. Why not? No, we couldn't. That was the right tactic, to take them from behind. We had no idea that the Russians were already in Germany. I was such an idiot back then. If, in that difficult time, when so much had to be thought through and overcome, if you got into a conflict about having done everything wrong – you didn't even want to admit it to yourself.

I think I've done a lot of things wrong in my life, and back then I didn't think about it. I belonged there; I was always very dutiful. You could rely on my work: that worked, that was right, and when I had a task I had to fulfil it. It's been like that my whole life, even then, whether the work was good or bad. That wasn't the main thing, whether I was working at the

Corporation or in the Propaganda Ministry – it was all the same stuff. It didn't make any difference. Back then you were just thinking: phew, I'm still alive. Even if everything at home was broken, you're still alive. Oh, the windows are broken again, the doors won't shut, but you're still alive. That was the thinking of thousands of people who lived with it every day. It was nothing; it was part of things, like breathing.

At any rate we were sitting there in that bunker like rats and the Russians were in Berlin. Suddenly two people from the Corporation building on Masurenallee turned up, people I knew. One of them was Hanne Sobek;[6] he was a footballer, before football became as important as it is today. He was one of the really brilliant footballers and he was given a job in the sport department at the Corporation. He and somebody else came on foot, and said that the Russians were already in Masurenallee. We were still sitting in the cellar. There was no phone; we no longer had a connection to the outside world and we were sitting in the cellar liked trapped mice.

We still had one of the most senior members of staff with us: that was Hans Fritzsche, and some of the advisors from the Propaganda Ministry were there as well. Hans Fritzsche was Berlin's Deputy Gauleiter, and in that capacity Herr Fritzsche was Goebbels's deputy. He was mostly busy with the other advisors, but then Herr Fritzsche gave us a task to do: we had to empty food sacks of flour and rice and noodles. They were separated out or cut open and we had to stitch together a huge white flag. We had nothing to stitch them with, but somehow we did it and made a flag. We also noticed that it had slowly become quieter in Berlin, and if you heard shots you noticed that they were rifle shots and not artillery shelling like before – it was small-arms fire. At any rate we stitched together that big flag, somehow. And Fritzsche, with two men beside him, said he would go, even though there was still constant shooting outside, and try to get down Bendlerstrasse to talk to the Russians. He set off with some other people, leaving us alone, but he said, 'Stay here, I'll look after you. We're taking the white flag to Bendlerstrasse.' That was where the Russians had their military high command.

When they'd been away for hours, a Russian crowd forced their way in. We were really a poor rabble and had no leaders any more. Herr Fritzsche, who we all liked a lot and valued, had left us in the lurch – so we really sat there like lambs to the slaughter. We were waiting for the Russians, and suddenly there they were. A squad of maybe five or six Russian soldiers. Mostly they had Mongolian faces – totally alien faces – and of course they had their rifles on their shoulders. They were scared themselves, forcing their way into a house like that, when there were so many corridors and so on. They were prepared to be attacked in one way or another. They crept down the corridor and then pushed the door open.

There were about ten of us. They drove us together and wanted to lead us out – force us out. We were already out of our underground hole, and then I heard another shot. Someone said, 'That was Meier'. We were driven out to the exit on to Mauerstrasse, which was the rear exit of the Propaganda Ministry. We were back in daylight for the first time in ten days; we were all green in the face, and all looked terrible. They were pushing us somewhere with their rifles, and I'm sure we thought it was all over. Then suddenly a squad came towards us from Mauerstrasse, with a white flag – torn, but still recognisable as a flag.

I can't remember if Fritzsche was still with them, but one of the men who had gone with him was there. He might even have been there himself. At any rate there were Russian officers at their head. We were pushed back into the bunker. We couldn't ask any questions; we were chess pieces being pushed back and forth. There we sat again, and Fritzsche wasn't there any more. Russian soldiers came, but they looked quite different this time. Stylish, with good suits; they came from military command, from Chuikov,[7] that was his name – the supreme commander in Berlin. After Fritzsche had seen him and agreed the surrender of the city of Berlin, he took charge of us, and these soldiers that he was sending now belonged to the elite. They dragged us out again and took us on foot from the city centre to Tempelhof.

Suddenly everything was deadly silent in Berlin, with just the sound of trotting horses. I only heard and saw a few car horns and trucks, but no more shooting. The city was still full of corpses that hadn't yet been cleared away. We weren't aware of anything any more. Russian women in uniforms had even been deployed to control the traffic.

We had to stop at a corner, and there was an elderly German couple there. They stood with us and looked at how we were surrounded by the soldiers, and asked, 'Have you been taken prisoner or what?' We said, 'We don't know yet.' And then the Russians started going 'Davai, davai' again and pushed us on and the other couple with us. The Russians wanted to get away quickly, so they simply pushed them into our group.

Near Tempelhof they pushed us into a little flat, a two-room flat. There must have been ten of us. So that's where we sat, and we spent a night there. There was nothing to eat, nothing to drink, nothing. That elderly couple was still with us, and they cried when they found out who they'd been thrown together with; they were in complete despair. There were a few Russians who spoke a bit of German, and we did all we could to make it clear to the Russians that this couple were complete strangers and had nothing to do with us – that they'd just wanted to cross the road at the corner and had been taken along by mistake. They actually let them go free; they believed us.

But then they wouldn't leave me alone, and the lady I was initially locked up with was a White Russian; her parents had fled Russia in 1918 after the great Revolution. There were a lot of White Russians living in Berlin, and for the Russians they were even worse than the Nazis, because they were actually traitors. Her husband was a journalist and they'd picked up her husband as well somewhere. They were constantly being called in for questioning, and the poor woman was badly tortured.

When I was arrested by the Russians I thought, 'The war's over now.' Now things will somehow get back to normal. The Russians who questioned me were also quite friendly; there were interpreters with good German. They were nice, I thought, they'll let me go home now. So I was still quite confident. When we were all sitting there in the room and due to be questioned, we discussed it all amongst ourselves. 'We'll just say we were going from one place to another and had just taken refuge from the shooting in the Propaganda Ministry.' Others said, 'No, no contradictions. One person saying one thing; another saying a different thing.'

I thought to myself: I'll tell the truth. I'll say I worked there. Of course only doing shorthand for that dreadful Dr Goebbels. I never saw him, because it's a big building after all, and I was far too unimportant. I never saw him, but I did work there. Before that I worked at the Broadcasting Corporation and was then compulsorily transferred to the Propaganda Ministry – which was true – and then I never saw him. It was all in my files at the time. Because I thought that if I was questioned and then questioned again – we read about things like that – then you'll slip up and they'll catch you lying. But as long as I always tell the truth I know I can stand by it and it won't be anything serious. They couldn't punish me for that. Anyway, I didn't think about suicide or being shot. They'll just let me go home. That's what I thought.

I didn't do anything, because it came out that they knew. They didn't say, 'Now we'll keep you here.' They said 'Thank you' and led me away again. And they didn't release me for five years.

Evil exists. The devil exists. God doesn't exist. But there is no justice.
Justice doesn't exist.

Brunhilde Pomsel

'WE KNEW NOTHING': ARREST
AND NEW BEGINNING

After her arrest, Brunhilde Pomsel ended up in Soviet Special Camp No. 2, which was set up in August 1945 on the site of the former Buchenwald concentration camp. The Soviet camp was organised on the order of the People's Commissar for Internal Affairs, Lavrenti Beria, and was almost completely isolated and used primarily for the internment of National Socialists and war criminals. Prisoners had no contact with their families and were otherwise cut off from any information from the outside world. Many prisoners died in the camp from illness and malnutrition.

Rejecting personal guilt, in her retrospective analysis Pomsel delivers her judgement on Joseph Goebbels and the regime.

If I had listened to Dr Collatz I wouldn't have ended up in that concentration camp and been dragged by the Russians from one camp to another. I should certainly have left Berlin. Our flat was wrecked, so I couldn't stay there. And now that was my fate. Who is in control of his fate in such agitated times? Very few people can say: I did this and this for that and that reason. It just happens to us! But now I had the bad luck to be picked up. If I had been in my wrecked flat, then I wouldn't have been in the Ministry, then the Russians wouldn't have come and found me. If I'd stayed at home, nothing at all might have happened.

Of course you've thought about whether there was something you could have done against the Nazis. It wasn't possible. Or it would have meant putting your life on the line. You had to expect the worst, and there were enough examples of that. It was all a huge crime, everyone was clear about that afterwards. But at the time… We were so wrapped in propaganda and we slipped into it. There was a large portion of stupidity involved as well, but part of it was that you had no connections. Who had any connections abroad in those days? Nobody.

And the few who tried to make a stand – what good did it do? None of them are alive any more. Many people hoped for something quite different from the state, and on recommendations they joined the Party and wanted to take part. The only people with a truly strong will to join the Party with intent and conviction were primarily the ones who were members of the SS, and of course the SA, but maybe not as much; the SA were more for the common people. The SS were to be treated with considerable caution.

However I found myself in the political cauldron, I was still an outsider. I don't think about it. I don't know how it could have been prevented, either. There will always be idiots who follow the wrong people, and pay dearly for it. In fact I can't imagine it happening again. But whether people learned from it – I don't know. After the end of the First World War Germany was leaderless. There were no personalities there, and that was why it was so easy for Hitler. Too many unemployed, and they were his whole support. Now we have a completely different form of government, a different way of life.

No, I don't think a thing like that will happen again; it wouldn't be possible now. Of course National Socialism could have been prevented. But in those days there were only extremes facing one another: the strong opposition between Communism and nationalism. That isn't so marked today.

It was only after my release that I found out what had happened. Other people in Germany had been slowly informed about things. After the end of the war and the Nuremberg Trials, they learned about all the things that had happened during that time. It's just as bad when you find out slowly, a little bit every day. You get used to it. When I found out about those things in the camp – about those images, those mass graves – I woke up to it. But it still wasn't our fault, if we didn't know about it. And it will never be my fault either. No. I myself was imprisoned in Buchenwald and Sachsenhausen and in a factory in East Berlin, which was occupied by the Russians, so I was never in a Russian prison, and even where I was we didn't learn anything about the things that had happened. We were isolated.

Where Goebbels was concerned – I only really understood the kind of people Goebbels and his wife must have been right at the end. They could have fled. Above all, I wonder why they had to kill themselves, and particularly the children. Yes, the Russians were there, but Hanna Reitsch[1] had offered to fly them out. Supposedly she could have landed her little plane to fly out the children. It's the attitude of the mother that I really don't understand. They also say – I don't remember, I heard it somewhere or other – that the eldest girl furiously resisted taking that pill. I think they were given a sleeping pill beforehand. The child is supposed to have known or guessed what was happening, and fought back. It's unimaginable.

Goebbels taking his own life – fine, he had no other option. But everything else is cowardice. Bringing the children into it – inexcusable! The children would have lived and become their own people. No, that's so brutal. A mother being able to kill the children she brought into the world, and such premeditated murder. There are sometimes excuses for spontaneous murder, but it's definitely as great a crime as the whole war. So people who caused this whole drama, who then made off like that and shifted responsibility to the next in line, they are craven cowards as far as I'm concerned. They swallow one of those pills and they're gone. Göring, bites the pill, gone. The others have to face the music. But the one who was ultimately responsible was right at the top – Hitler.

I'd known for some time that there were concentration camps, but that people were gassed and burned in them – never. If I imagine standing under something like that in Buchenwald when we were led to the showers... You had to take off your clothes and hang them on a hook – mine was hook number 47 – and while I was showering my clothes were cleaned and then hung in another room on a hook with the same number, so that I could find them again. Meanwhile I stood for a quarter of an hour in a big tiled room, where there were big showers placed at regular intervals. The water came out, and you stood under it, and it bubbled out nicely. You got a little bit of soap so that you could wash yourself and everything. The shower was warm for a really long time – until it turned cold, and then out you went into that other warm room, it was always nice and warm. Then you got dressed and left again. Afterwards I felt ill at the idea that in the same place – which we always looked forward to because we had warm water on our skin again at last – that these things were used to pump out gas to kill the Jews. I don't know exactly how they did it, but that's how they killed them.

But I felt I was being treated very badly and very wrongly, that I of all people should have been taken away by the Russians. Because all I had done was type in Herr Goebbels's office. No, so I can't bring myself to feel a sense of guilt. I'm guilty if I do something. All I did was have the bad luck not to be at home on the day when the Russians went to the Propaganda Ministry.

But of course I'm guilty in the sense of being stupid. But it wasn't what everybody wanted. They promised themselves a new revival after the loss of the First World War, and at first that actually happened. A re-blossoming of a humiliated people who had lost the war and not gained some of the rights that could have grown out of the Treaty. The people who knew most about the atrocities were the ones who were in direct contact with the institutions and the prisons, and they didn't speak out, for fear that they themselves might have to pay the price. They weren't even always Party members. Many of them were simple, plain, perhaps slightly stupid, at least politically stupid people, who didn't think about it all very much.

I wasn't one of them; I would have had to know a lot more than I did. It was more or less out of thoughtlessness that I joined that stupid Party that most people were in, but then imprisonment turned out to be a mixed blessing. At first I was terribly afraid when the Russians had crossed the German border – afraid of what they were doing to German women. All of that was unthinkable for us.

But it didn't happen, and no one at the time knew where we were all headed. But after the war most people didn't know what they were going to live on. The companies that paid their wages had gone bust. Money no longer had any value. I just remember that in the summer of 1945 we sat outside the barracks in the former Buchenwald concentration camp. We didn't have to work, we just sat around and talked about home, and what it would be like, how things would go on. I remember once saying, 'At least with the Russians we get our pearl barley soup morning, noon and evening. Who knows whether our people at home always get enough to eat.' We had no information about how other people in Germany were faring.

We went through ups and downs as well. Even in Buchenwald I had lovely moments that I will never forget. I stood on the stage in a primitive little play written by an inmate and encouraged by a very nice Russian captain, who unfortunately stopped being camp commandant after that. He was replaced, although by a very nice man who was friendly towards the Germans, and who did an awful lot for the prisoners. In Buchenwald the Nazis had set up a real theatre, a stage with an orchestra pit for favoured prisoners at the time, and also for the people who worked there so that they got a bit of entertainment. The camp commandant sorted all of that out. At first, for his Russian soldiers, his guards, he put on little clownish skits, dressing up, things from circus acts, a bucket of soapy water over the head, that sort of thing.

You must realise that there were people like Heinrich George in the camp. We had a director from the Nollendorf Theater who was an inmate, and we had people from the Philharmonic, orchestra people, and the Russians supplied them with instruments. They just went out and took violins and flutes from private individuals and brought them to the camp to put together a wonderful band. It was primarily meant for the Russian soldiers, but more and more German things crept into it.

The camp commandant allowed the theatre director to rehearse a German play. Eight days before it was to be performed, one member of the theatre group, a female prisoner, was caught with a Russian soldier. The soldier was sent away and the girl was immediately removed from the theatre troupe, so the play had no lead and they needed a substitute at very short notice. I was asked if I was able to learn it by heart. 'Of course I can!' I said.

In the camp of course you had thoughts about things. Another year gone by, and you're still here. What will I do when I go home? Will I be able to do a job again? I already had one. I had to help out in a tailor's workshop organised by the Russians. I wasn't inactive for long.

Meanwhile I was often very lucky. I came back in January 1950 and threw my hand over my mouth when I heard about everything that had happened. Suddenly there was a new radio station, and they even took me on as a secretary. When I came back I thought at first I might be able to start at the station RIAS Berlin. No, they certainly wouldn't be taking on any former Nazis. You worked in the Propaganda

Ministry, you're a Nazi. Fine, then I'm a Nazi. But they made no exceptions. But then I ended up at Südwestfunk, as some people there knew me from before. They were former workers who had reported in propaganda units and about the war, and were already back at work. I don't remember exactly everyone who managed to get out of the Propaganda Ministry. Kurt Frowein managed, but I never saw him again, and Naumann too. He was with the Führer in the headquarters until the end, and he managed to get out of Berlin with Martin Bormann[2] and Schwägermann.

Dr Naumann contacted me when I was already in Baden-Baden. 'Dear Fräulein Pomsel, I am glad that you were one of those who survived that terrible war, and that you are doing well again and have found a very nice job in the Südwestfunk. I would be very happy if you would contact me. I have met up with some very good friends again.' Naumann had also met Werner Titze, who was the editor-in-chief at Südwestfunk and a schoolmate of Naumann's; they were both born in Görlitz and probably met up again by chance in Bonn. Then they ran through the people from the Reich Broadcasting Corporation and the Propaganda Ministry, who they knew or didn't know, and my name came up.

Luckily I went to my former boss, Lothar Hartmann, the director of programmes, with whom I later went to Munich. I asked him what he thought about it and he advised me against contacting Naumann. So I didn't, and just a few days later I read in *Der Spiegel* that he was involved in a conspiracy to infiltrate the liberal FDP [Free Democratic Party]. He was still a Nazi. I never heard of him again. They were all a few years older than I was, and they're all dead now. It comes up again and again in the papers. Someone turns up Nazis who worked in German law courts even later on, after the war. Many people were very skilled at shaking off responsibility. I didn't understand that, and I didn't see any reason to do it either.

I really found out about the most terrible things only after I came out of prison – about the extent of the persecution of the Jews and the camps. Until my release I didn't speak to anybody, no relatives, no colleagues, nobody. I was in the hands of the Russians, and that was that. Everything that came after – the Nuremberg Trials, a new currency, the GDR [German Democratic Republic] – I only found out about that when I came home in 1950, put twenty-four marks on the table in front of my mother and said, 'Mama, that's what I've earned in five years.' They had paid me that on the last day, in fact. My mother said, 'Child, you can throw that in the waste-paper basket, that's Eastern money.'

There are funny details I remember. At my first dinner: 'Mama, since when have we always eaten white bread?' She said, 'White bread, that isn't white bread.' It was normal bread, but for me it was white bread. Can you imagine what we got in the camp, it was black bread, but what black bread! For me this was a completely new, altered world.

When I was being questioned I was also asked if I had a cyanide capsule on me somewhere. Nobody ever offered me one. I would have accepted it, but not for me. I didn't plan to take my life. But perhaps I would have taken it in Sachsenhausen; I'd really reached my limit there. It was three months before I was released. I had a knife, which you weren't supposed to have. A blunt knife. I clearly remember playing about with that knife and thinking, how do you open your veins? But a blunt knife isn't going to be much use. So I only played with the idea, and then I put it away again and thought to myself, 'No, no, I'm not going to do anything as stupid as that.' Basically I don't tend to throw in the towel that quickly. I remember a secretary of the Führer's writing about how proud she was to have been given a capsule like that by Hitler, but no girl from the Propaganda Ministry made it over to the Führer's bunker.

I was often very lucky. Sooner or later there was always a way out. I was often in a state of despair, but somehow or other it always passed and let me become what I am now. Of course I'm no longer that naive little girl who finds the world great fun. I've encountered the world from all sides, from many sides.

Then there was Eva Löwenthal, who was never out of my head. What had become of her? Only decades later, visiting a cemetery in Berlin, I found out what had happened to her. I looked around the cemetery and went to one of the attendants to ask whether she might be among the missing. I only had her name and her approximate age. 'I'm missing someone called Eva Löwenthal,' I said. He went to a machine with a list of names, and we found her, a year older or a year younger than me. According to the list she had died, and it also gave the year: it was right at the end of the war, early in 1945. We couldn't find out anything more than that.

Eva had always sat at the table with the rest of us. She was part of it. She was an intelligent girl: she had read a lot, and she often made me feel stupid. I thought: you with your basic education. And now she was actually dead. At the time I couldn't grasp it. The persecution of the Jews hadn't been as active in my district as in others. Most had left in time – they had money and connections abroad. But mostly they kept themselves to themselves. They were self-contained. For example, the circle of acquaintances of my boss Dr Goldberg, who invited me to his little parties, that was the whole clan of the Leiser shoe manufacturing company. They bred like rabbits, bringing lots of children into the world. They didn't even allow their financial interests to merge with those of other people. And as for schooling, most of the Jewish children attended private schools.

Eva was someone special as far as we were concerned. We knew she needed a bit of protection, and she had no money. She couldn't even apply for a job. When you applied for a job you had to reveal what faith community you belonged to. That was how it was. But those differences also existed among the Jews. There were a lot of poor Jews too, like Rosa Lehmann Oppenheimer. She had that little shop selling soap. I liked going there as a child. Her shop always smelled of paraffin, and she herself did too. Still, when she reached into the big sweetie jar with her hand, which wasn't always very clean, and then pressed a whole handful of unwrapped sweets in your hand, of course she was the loveliest person in the world. Rosa Lehmann Oppenheimer... She was taken away, I was told later. She was one of the poor Jews. They existed too.

After Hitler came to power it was too late for everything...
Brunhilde Pomsel

'I WASN'T GUILTY': THE CV OF A 103-YEAR-OLD WOMAN

It's like everything else. Even beautiful things have stains. And terrible things have bright spots. It's not all black and white. There's always a bit of grey in both.

I never went along with the crowd. I was only in the crowd when I did gymnastics, when I went on jaunts, when I played bridge – then we were a delightful crowd. I'm essentially a loner; I've never married or brought children into the world. Not because I have anything against marriage, and I would have liked to have a child, but in the old days you couldn't have a child without being married. It would have been a scandal, and I never wanted to expose myself to that.

But I like being alone – I always have done. I think I had that desire even as a child, when I didn't have my own room. Always with the boys, and it was always so cramped. I wanted to be alone a lot, but I also liked spending a lot of time with nice people. It might be selfishness of some kind. But at least it wasn't selfishness at other people's expense, because of course you were part of a crowd in spite of everything. I'm not that kind of individualist. As long as I can do the things that fulfil or inspire me, and don't have the feeling that I'm bothered by the crowd, I'm happy to get involved. If I hadn't been at the Propaganda Ministry, the story would have been exactly the same. It's not just about me on my own.

Every individual belongs somewhere. Of course! There's always an influence of some kind. Sometimes it's upbringing, sometimes the circle you're part of; I don't know. In Germany before Hitler came to power life wasn't particularly open. It was a completely different world back then. Many people nowadays can't even imagine that restricted life. It starts with the upbringing of children: if they were badly behaved they got the slipper. Love and understanding didn't get you very far. From a clip around the ear to trousers down, three smacks and that was it – and you didn't resent it.

Who in those days had friends in America or anywhere? A schoolfriend of mine trained as a hairdresser, and even as an apprentice she was lucky enough to be able to travel on the *Bremen*, an amazing ship that travelled between Germany and America. She was envied for having such a great job. None of us knew any foreigners. At first there was no broadcasting, not to mention all the other technical nonsense that they have today. Nothing. We were still living on an island – not just us, other countries were exactly the same. There wasn't that network, except in trade, and that was a separate class. We were undeveloped. Today, no one could hope to escape the modern world.

I expect young people or the next generation just think sensibly about these things. Of course we're always subject to certain influences. At a certain age most people are enthusiastic, and they commit themselves to something – but it doesn't last. Afterwards, when life becomes more serious for them and they have to assume responsibility, perhaps they even want to have a family, then it slowly stops. What happened back then only happens when you have discontented crowds. They have time to take to the streets.

I never used to take an interest in politics. Now that I'm older I'm more interested in political developments. Before, there were more important things for me to think about – personal things. Germany was punished for its national ego and its deeds; for its negligence, and its apathy. I don't think that could happen very much these days.

It's hard when you've passed through a period like that, a trough like that. In the end, however, it is still my only life, my fate and in the end everyone only thought about themselves. Sometimes I get a bit of a guilty conscience, sometimes it's your own fault, and then I think: you actually came out of it well every time. I knew more about those terrible, ugly things than the average person. But I always survived that too. If I was a young person now I would do things differently from the way I did them before. Things start much earlier than they did. Not least young people getting involved in everything, like broadcasting and television.

Perhaps these days we have more control of our own fate. Everything in me revolts against the improbability that there's someone who decides our fate; it's a gruesome idea. That there is a personality – God – who decides that such terrible things should happen. I'm not thinking about what happened to me. I was only unlucky, but nothing was terrible. On the contrary, I sometimes made things difficult for myself by being sensitive. Some people criticised me for my big nose. Sometimes they either didn't see me at all – I was so small and inconspicuous – but people liked me all the more the better they got to know me. At least that's what I imagine. I also had an inferiority complex in various ways. But I do have a certain confidence, I admit I've got that. I think I'm a good comrade.

I've also done a lot of good in my life. Assuming I'd married and had children... I don't know, you can't say what kind of partner you would have had. I wouldn't have been able to think as much about myself as I have done. I've fulfilled many of the desires that many people have to forgo because of illness, children, unhappy marriages and so on. That's also made me a little cowardly; I haven't been inclined to take risks. I've got a certain caution and a certain cunning. I'm not proud of anything, but in retrospect I'm always glad when I've done something. I'm not the kind of person who absolutely has to make something happen, but when I've succeeded with something: well, if I'm content, that's a nice state to be in.

But I answered that constant question of guilt early on. No, I don't feel guilty. Absolutely not. Why would I? Now, I wouldn't describe myself as guilty. Unless you're going to accuse the whole German people of helping that government come to power in the end. That was all of us, including me.

It was never my personal wish to go to the Propaganda Ministry. It was an order, a compulsory instruction, and no one can imagine what that meant at the time. I was ordered to go there. I didn't apply for it. It was a transfer, and I had to go along with it. If I'd said, I don't want to, they'd have said, 'What do you mean you don't want to? That's not an option.'

Clearly in the department that I belonged to, the current affairs department in the Corporation, there was no work left in 1942. There were spin-offs, when staff members who were also housewives brought the vegetables that they'd planted and harvested in their gardens into the office, and since they had no bosses and weren't getting any dictation, they chopped the beans and filled their preserving jars and then carried them home again on their bicycles. So it wasn't hard for me to leave the department. My men from the Corporation were all gone. All gone. They were all in the war. The lucky ones were in Paris, and none of them forgot me. We all dreamed of getting back together when the war was over.

I had to earn money somehow, and it had all been very respectable and decent. Ending up in the Propaganda Ministry was all a bit naive on my part. I sometimes was a bit naive. But I don't feel guilty – and if I did, I would have repaid my debt a million times.

I don't think people will be so stupid as to fall for that again. I can't imagine it. I mean, I'm still aware of the crowd as a crowd. But I also see people being very sluggish and a bit lazy about thinking and being critical. As long as they've got enough to eat, everything's fine. If someone takes care of some of their concerns – that happens sometimes in politics. And if not? Who knows!

I sometimes wonder how young people – these are observations that I've made from watching television – how they deal with such problems. We didn't do that. Not at all. They all seem much more mature to me, and I'm very much aware of that. I wish our own upbringing had been like that, but we had to be more obedient in those days, and things are more relaxed about punishment and sometimes strictness. Everything works better, there is more order. Whether that's worth striving for is a whole different question. Very often when I see young people on television, school students, debating, I think: my God, what confidence they have, an ability to engage with the life that lies ahead of them.

We were stupid in those days. There wasn't time to think about everything – ordinary people would be thinking about when they had to go to work. In my circle we were largely untouched by problems. They didn't burden or preoccupy us, the way they preoccupy me now that my life is behind me. I'm much more interested in them now. I'm just trying to explain to you how as a young person who is simply released into life there seems to be some kind of direction. But it doesn't always need to be an influence. That's easier to observe in the present day.

Today on television I saw school students who were trying to persuade strangers about the coming elections. I admired the boys and girls; they were about sixteen years old. The older people were often very dismissive: I'm not interested, stop bothering me or things like that. They just ignored them. Those young people were so eager as they approached old and elderly people and tried to point out problems to them. They didn't have things like that in the old days. We were left to our own devices. Unless you joined the scouts or the German Girls' League. Personally I didn't want anything to do with any of that. I didn't want anything with a uniform, marching with the crowd.

I'm someone who is able to think the way young people think. I have a lot in common with them. I'm not one of those adults who see children as know-alls, or not mature enough to make a judgement about things. I think children are aware of a great many things; sometimes they don't even need to be ten years old if they fall into the right hands, so you can tell what's going on in their minds. If I just think about my own upbringing, I can't imagine my father ever discussing such matters with us. We were never allowed to know what party he voted for. There were elections often enough. We always wanted to know, 'How did you vote?' And he would always say, 'That's none of your business!'

You can't do that. If things had been different, I might have developed differently as well and I might have wanted to become something more responsible and paid more attention to who or what I was working for, what I was getting into. I was always very frisky and a bit shallow. Well, it helped me too. My nature!

Today I can see that that was all very superficial. Before, there was no Propaganda Ministry, and now there is no Propaganda Ministry and the world doesn't miss it either. It was an absolute invention on the part of those crazy Nazis. They were the worst kind of egoists. There was no love of the fatherland, none of that. Only egoism – quite terrible, not a trace of idealism. I didn't know any of that in those days. But I don't feel guilty about any of it. I didn't do anything; I don't feel guilty. All the many people who were often disparaged as

Nazis — what are the people as a whole? It's like a sea, every-one together. It's a constant movement back and forth.

Only certain personalities had an effect on me. Those gener-alisations, like the guilt of the German people — that's all non-sense. We are guided by a certain class of egoists. Sometimes they are gentler, sometimes more brutal. If you think back on history, what the ruling class did in the past; I can't imagine anyone would deliberately accept something like that, become an advocate of those things. That's not what I am trying to do. But who can know everything?

I may have worked with more criminals in my life than I know. You don't know that beforehand. During the time when I was working for Goebbels, of course he was one of the big bosses right at the top as far as I was concerned; for me he came just after Hitler. And the orders came to me from the Ministry, as they did for every soldier who fired at Russian, French or English soldiers, and that doesn't make them mur-derers. They were doing their duty. I could really only reproach myself if I had unjustly hurt somebody very badly, and I can't remember doing that.

Simply speaking, there was nothing we could do. After 1933 it was too late. Of course, I could have gone to see Eva Löwenthal every day and helped her, but she wasn't as close to me as all that, and we couldn't really help her anyway. If she smoked away the little that she earned rather than at least going to buy something to eat, then we can't help her, we thought. We were very quick to judge. The example of Eva is only supposed to bring clarity. There will have been many examples of friends who went on supporting Jews.

Some people even put themselves in danger – as we know from everything we discovered later. But people today who claim they would have done more for the poor persecuted Jews back then – I'm even willing to believe that they are honest about it when they say it now, but they wouldn't have done it. After the Nazis were in power, it was as if the whole country was under a bell jar. We were all in a huge concentration camp. After Hitler came to power it was too late for everything, and everyone had his own personal issues to deal with, and not just the persecution of the Jews. There was so much else as well. There were the many fates of one's own relatives who were at war. But that isn't supposed to excuse anything.

Apart from the Nazis themselves – the leaders of this movement, who worked with false, completely false prophecies – it is the indifference of the people that made it all possible. I'm not trying to link that with individuals by any means. The indifference of people, which you see over and over again. That we are really in a position to see on television how this terrible story is playing out in Syria, hundreds of people drowning, and then there's a variety show. We don't change our lives because of it. I think that's just how it is in life. Everything is all mixed up.

The best thing that you can blame some people for: they were idealists in those days, and so blind in their faith that they really believed Germany was on the way up. Because by then we were a people who lived very modestly. They believed that; I'm sure there were a lot of people who believed out of a true love of the fatherland, out of genuine conviction, that a group of men, by taking charge of everything, would do everything better.

If I had been able to guess or know everything back then, I certainly wouldn't have gone to the Broadcasting Corporation or the Propaganda Ministry. For me, Goebbels was a politician who tended to shout a bit loudly. I didn't think about it at all. I also never listened to all that codswallop, his speeches. Everyone was saying the same things. I don't listen to speeches in the Bundestag either. It's all just claptrap, what they come out with.

I can't give any advice to young people today. I don't need to influence anybody, I don't need to affect anybody, I have no obligations, I can think for myself, whatever I want. If someone just lives for themselves and has no interest in these subjects then he doesn't exist. It's a bit different if you live in a community; a community is a kind of family. Or if you're younger and you have more friends that you can talk to. But I'm now excluded from all of that. Here I can't talk to anybody any more, and if I have visitors – well, we talk about other things, even today. But blind obedience is a bad thing in every situation. In certain matters you must obey, of course, but you can't just say yes for the sake of comfort.

I have never had children, but if I had I would have made them get involved very early on. We were brought up too much to be obedient people. You are of course very dependent on the circumstances you grow up in, the way everything develops – develops outwardly, and politically, in a human sense. I'm coming to terms with everything as it is now. I sometimes envy people who can always find comfort in their faith. I don't have that. I always say it's chance, anything that I myself didn't bring about is pure chance. People today are offered so many possibilities that they can get confused. They can't always tell if everything they're offered is a real opportunity or not.

I do have one piece of advice, though. Something that doesn't exist in practical life: there is no justice. There isn't even any justice in the legal system. To begin with, opinions about all kinds of things change, and they're in constant flux. In the past homosexuals were either something laughed at or said 'Ugh!' about. Now they're even having children. It doesn't surprise me at all.

So much happens in life that you couldn't even have imagined fifty years ago. I've always thought that I can learn, but now I find it hard to use my mobile phone; I've got so stupid in the meantime. Sometimes I wonder why I've grown so old after all I've been through. I'm such a weak old thing who can't push gates open and can't really see any more and can't really walk because I can't really see. And it's still not over. I sometimes wonder whether I'll die in my sleep, maybe when I go to sleep. I can't imagine dying of an illness. I think I'll go in my sleep. But I really don't care.

After the filming in 2013, in November 2016 Brunhilde Pomsel gave another glimpse into a personal conflict that perhaps reveals a very individual aspect of repression as a survival strategy, and which was also presumably no less crucial for the overall picture of being unwilling to look, and just getting on with the job.

Before the 1936 Olympic Games she met Gottfried Kirchbach in a pub in Berlin. Gottfried Kirchbach was a German print-maker and illustrator, born in Munich in 1888 and the son of the German painter Frank Kirchbach. Among other things, he worked for the Propaganda Stuttgart advertising agency and designed election posters, for example for the SPD and the USPD. He had a Jewish mother, and therefore was a half-Jew by the racial laws of the National Socialists. He knew very well from the stories of Brunhilde Pomsel what the plans were for the Jews, even though he himself had not suffered any reprisals. He also knew what position Brunhilde Pomsel was in at the Reich Broadcasting Corporation, but the two of them barely spoke of those matters. Without reveal-ing any further details from the everyday life of that relationship under the strict racial laws, Pomsel describes how after the 1936 Olympic Games Kirchbach moved to Amsterdam to escape persecu-tion by the Nazis. Brunhilde Pomsel was ready to follow him with packed suitcases, but he turned against the idea; he first had to sort out his life in Amsterdam so that he could look after a family. A pregnant Brunhilde Pomsel was left behind, but had to termin-ate the pregnancy on the advice of her doctor, as her lung disease made the prospect of giving birth to the child too dangerous. She describes it as a painful process. She and Kirchbach saw each other a few more times in Amsterdam before it became too dangerous for her to keep taking regular trips without arousing the suspicion of the authorities. After the outbreak of war contact was severed and she never saw her lover again. Gottfried Kirchbach died in Amsterdam in 1942. For the rest of her life Brunhilde Pomsel lived alone and childless. She died in Munich the night before International Holocaust Remembrance Day on 27 January 2017 at the age of 106.

WHAT THE STORY OF GOEBBELS'S SECRETARY TEACHES US FOR THE FUTURE

Thore D. Hansen

More than almost any eyewitness of the Nazi regime, Brunhilde Pomsel openly admits to her opportunism; she places her own advantage – her youthful egoism – in the foreground in order to explain her lack of interest in politics and her later role in National Socialism. The experience of poverty, the fear of social decline and a longing for affluence and advancement run through her childhood and youth to her adulthood. Her professional progress was the most important thing to her, and she preferred to look away rather than to engage with the deeds of her boss Joseph Goebbels and try to find a way out for herself.

Goebbels was one of the main architects of National Socialism. Film and radio, the new developments of the 1930s for reaching the masses, were deployed for propaganda purposes and for the indoctrination of the German people, and particularly for the defamation of Jews, Communists and other marginal groups. Goebbels's anti-Semitic propaganda was the ideological preparation for the later Holocaust of the Jews. Even today, his speeches are considered exemplary in terms of how they manipulated the population.

You might ask incredulously: how can a young woman who lost her lover and a good friend because of political circumstances not see clearly the man she worked for? She carried on with a sense of duty and an extreme distortion of the facts, before ending up as a prisoner in a special Soviet camp standing under a shower not dissimilar to the one under which her friend Eva Löwenthal was presumably gassed. And yet she doesn't appear to grasp exactly what happened.

At the premiere of the documentary film *A German Life* viewers and journalists warned against all-out condemnation of the aged former secretary of Joseph Goebbels. They did this in the awareness that, even in our own times, ignorance, passivity and apathy have spread in the population, while other parts of society are becoming radicalised. Paul Garbulski of *Vice* magazine summed it up: 'I have always tried to protect myself from others, and it is the ordinary person in me, filled with sufficient weary absurdity, who paves the way for betrayal and the violence of entire armies. Let us pay attention to the little bit of Pomsel within each of us.'[1]

Brunhilde Pomsel tells us how she became what she is through her childhood memories. She was born in Berlin in 1911, the daughter of a decorator. She describes her frugal life after the First World War and the global economic crisis in the 1930s. Even though her family was relatively well off, she felt a growing yearning for affluence and a career. She was shaped by the child-rearing methods and strictness of her father. If one of the five children was badly behaved, they were smacked without further ado.

> … love and understanding didn't get you very far. Obedience and a bit of cheating, fibbing or shifting the blame on to someone else were also involved.

The National Socialists immediately put the blame for the state of Germany in the 1930s on to a concrete group – the Jews. Brunhilde Pomsel has a clear answer for those who claim today that they would definitely have acted on behalf of the Jews:

> But people today who claim they would have done more for the poor persecuted Jews back then – I'm even willing to believe that they are honest about it when they say it now, but they wouldn't have done it. After the Nazis were in power, it was as if the whole country was under a bell jar. We were all in a huge concentration camp. After Hitler came to power it was too late for everything, and everyone had his own personal issues to deal with, and not just the persecution of the Jews. There was so much else as well. There were the many fates of one's own relatives who were at war. But that isn't supposed to excuse anything.

In response to the question of how Hitler's rise to power in the 1920s should be explained, and why it wasn't possible to stop him, there is agreement in only one respect: there are no simple explanations. It was neither ideology and propaganda alone, nor Hitler's suggestive power, nor the terror of the SA in the streets or political and social circumstances, nor simply the humiliation of the Germans by the Versailles Treaty or the Communist threat or mass unemployment. None of these circumstances on its own explains the National Socialist rise to power, but taken together all of those factors had a deadly effect.

Immediately after the Second World War, the chief concern among the architects of the new constitutions in Germany, Italy or even Austria was to ensure that the new democratic systems could not be undermined by extremist movements, and that history could not repeat itself. As probably the last eyewitness from within the Nazi power apparatus, Brunhilde Pomsel gives us the opportunity to understand why rightwing populists, authoritarian systems and dictatorships are reappearing in the twenty-first century, why this has been occurring on an international level for a long time, and what the causes for it might be. It would be premature to claim that history is repeating itself, but it is as inappropriate as it is negligent to ignore the many indications that feed the fear that Europe might finally collapse – something that could give rise to military conflict.

If we look at Brunhilde Pomsel's most harmless and banal-sounding memories and reasons for her rise in National Socialism, there are comparisons with the present day. Large parts of the population of Western democracies can barely be bothered with facts, and tend to be driven by emotion. A sense of injustice can radicalise entire population groups, and in the end it only takes the creation of a suitable image of an enemy to win these groups over for simple solutions. The story of Brunhilde Pomsel can be seen as an example of the need to argue for the preservation of an open society.

For long passages during Pomsel's descriptions, one has the feeling that she is not expressing herself honestly. Certainly she has attempted to repress details of her work – and yet her knowledge of what was happening in the Propaganda Ministry lingered inside her for decades afterwards.

It's hard when you've passed through a period like that, a trough like that. In the end, however, it is still my only life, my fate and in the end everyone only thought about themselves. Sometimes I get a bit of a guilty conscience, sometimes it's your own fault, and then I think: you actually came out of it well every time. I knew more about those terrible, ugly things than the average person.

She tells us very little in precise terms about anything more concrete she might have learned. If Brunhilde Pomsel actually 'didn't know' anything, it's not because she *couldn't* have known but because she *didn't want* to know.

We didn't want to know much; we didn't want to burden ourselves even more unnecessarily. It was enough that we had to do battle with a lot of difficult things, since food supplies were getting worse and worse [...]

I was such an idiot back then. If, in that difficult time, when so much had to be thought through and overcome, if you got into a conflict about having done everything wrong – you didn't even want to admit it to yourself.

What she could have known has been amply covered elsewhere; we could hardly have expected new facts about the history of National Socialism from conversations with Pomsel, as she didn't want to talk about details or couldn't remember anything. What makes her statements so valuable for our own times can be found between the lines – because in spite of all the gaps in her memory, she has in the end reflected upon her life. In a certain sense she has delivered an unusual and sometimes apparently harsh confession about her role.

But of course I'm guilty in the sense of being stupid. But it wasn't what everybody wanted. They promised themselves a new revival after the loss of the First World War, and at first that actually happened. A re-blossoming of a humiliated people who had lost the war and not gained some of the rights that could have grown out of the Treaty.

When Brunhilde Pomsel claims to have known nothing about the true extent of the persecution of the Jews, we could rightly point out that she of all people, working in the Propaganda Ministry, where facts are embellished and news suppressed or invented, could very easily have known all kinds of things if she had wanted to. From 1942 rumours were spreading across the whole of the Reich that the Jews were not being resettled but were being put in concentration camps. Anonymous surveys even into the 1990s among eyewitnesses of the last century revealed that up to 40 per cent of the German population knew about the Holocaust before the end of the war. But Pomsel could also have looked unobserved through the files dealing with the trials against the White Rose or other trials at the notorious People's Court, rather than putting them in the safe unseen and being proud to have followed the instructions of her superior and thus gained his trust. The desire for personal recognition and her blind sense of duty towards her superior took precedence in the young secretary.

> It was a bit of an elite. That was why it was very nice working there. Everything was pleasant; I liked it. Nicely dressed people, friendly people. Yes, I was very superficial in those days, very stupid.

Her superficiality at the time is the only criticism she makes of herself here, while she dismisses any idea of personal guilt for the crimes of National Socialism. She would only accept such a thing if you

> accuse the whole German people of helping that government come to power in the end. That was all of us, including me.

This attitude of course ignores the fact that everyone must be ultimately answerable for his own decisions and his position in society, both then and now. But Brunhilde Pomsel's assessment is correct in terms of the result, because without the support of large numbers of the population for the Nazis, along with a simultaneous lack of interest in the true goals of the 'movement', presumably history would have been different in the 1930s.

Is a lack of interest in politics a fault in itself? As far as the question of the lessons that we can learn from her biography for our own time goes, it does not even matter whether she was a convinced National Socialist or not. She clearly wasn't. Between actively joining in and actively looking away the question of her guilt blurs into a self-protective assertion of personal stupidity and naivety. From a moral point of view, looking away is a fault, because life always means living with others. That is true, not least in a democracy in which universal human rights are an essential pillar of fundamental rights. But currently many people are turning away from the democratic system because they do not question the mechanisms that lead to the breakdown of social and human solidarity – or perhaps because they don't want to question them? In Pomsel's life, or at least so it seems, little mattered apart from her own advancement.

And now that was my fate. Who is in control of his fate in such agitated times? Very few people can say: I did this and this for that and that reason. It just happens to us!

Hitler's secretary Traudl Junge claimed to have known nothing about the Holocaust, and the telephone operator of the Führer's Escort Command, Rochus Misch, said many times that he never heard anything about the 'Final Solution' in the presence of Adolf Hitler. Common to them all is the fact that in the end they were either ashamed of their past, took no responsibility for it or hid away from it.

Even now there is barely any direct information on how the so-called 'Final Solution' was really discussed in Joseph Goebbels's circle of staff members. Even if it were true that only Joseph Goebbels's personal advisors, not the secretaries, knew about plans for the destruction of the Jews in Europe, it is still difficult to put much faith in Brunhilde Pomsel's claim that she knew nothing about it. Since the notes for Goebbels's diktats, which have been passed down to us, are not initialled, it is now impossible to tell who recorded them. But it is very hard to imagine that a secretary working at the top level wouldn't have known what was going on.[2]

There are many accusations that might be levelled against Pomsel. She apparently distances herself from her own past, perhaps because she wants to examine her unconscious guilt at having been there. She had almost seventy years to come to terms with things. The fact is that she served a man who seduced and manipulated a whole people and drove them into the abyss. She repeatedly and definitively denies any personal guilt in the crimes of National Socialism and also insists that she knew nothing about them, perhaps making it easier for her to deal with the truth. For long stretches she succeeds in doing this far more successfully than many other servants of the Nazi leadership managed to do after the war when they tried to cleanse, deny or even just whitewash their biographies.

I may have worked with more criminals in my life than I know. You don't know that beforehand. During the time when I was working for Goebbels, of course he was one of the big bosses right at the top as far as I was concerned; for me he came just after Hitler. And the orders came to me from the Ministry, as they did for every soldier who fired at Russian, French or English soldiers, and that doesn't make them murderers. They were doing their duty. I could really only reproach myself if I had unjustly hurt somebody very badly, and I can't remember doing that.

Her story gives us the opportunity to see what happens when the emergence of a dictatorship is ignored and later what it means to live (or survive) in that dictatorship – both physically and mentally. But it also makes clear what it means to watch today's populists strive to bring an end to Western-style democracy. Pomsel, who died in January 2017 at the age of 106, should interest us because her openly expressed 'cowardice' and apolitical attitude reveal something that has been flourishing for some time even today: a great indifference, or a political weariness and apathy towards the fate of refugees; a blazing hatred directed against democratic elites; and the new rise of right-wing populists, who have declared war on democracy and European integration. Her unreflective egoism and the enticing job offer from Wulf Bley as well as the desire to rise through the ranks and to belong were major reasons for her joining the Party and the Broadcasting Corporation. That's how she *slipped into it*.

It was thanks to that lucky encounter with Wulf Bley that I had a contract, and a very nice contract too. Oh, I can't remember how much exactly now, but anyway I was making over 200 marks a month. That was crazy money. Compared with what I had got by on for years, it was a princely sum. At first I worked for the board of directors, and then in the office of the former directors. That wasn't terribly honourable in itself, because there were people there who were due to be shunted off – all the secretaries who had been senior in the former Broadcasting Corporation. They had worked for the Jews, because most of the board members had been Jews, who had all been thrown out or sent to the camps; or at any rate out of the broadcasting centre.

In search of parallels between the 1930s and the present day we inevitably find ourselves confronting certain questions: what is happening in Europe and the United States? Are parts of the population, most of whom have not yet been radicalised by the new demagogues, in the end just as passive, ignorant or indifferent towards current developments as Pomsel described herself and those around her when she was aged twenty-two to thirty-four? Is youth today just as apolitical, and is the political disenchantment of the middle class the actual threat to democracy? Have the democratic elites failed by ignoring the long-term consequences and causes of an increasing political disenchantment? Are we returning, open-eyed, through our passive attitude and apathy, to the 1930s? And can we really draw conclusions for the present day from Pomsel's biography – conclusions that will stir us into action? Anyone who does not wish to see totalitarian states emerging should take the experience of the 1930s and Brunhilde Pomsel's life story seriously.

In our own times we are seeing a dictatorship emerging in Turkey. In the end it is people like Brunhilde Pomsel who have, at the behest of President Recep Tayyip Erdoğan, brought the opposition, parliament and the media under the sole control of the president to ensure Erdoğan's power. We don't know how much opportunism these police officers, functionaries and other henchmen displayed or had to display just to live (or survive) in Erdoğan's new system, but they are calling democracy into question.

In the south-east of Turkey, according to estimates from Amnesty International, within a year, as a consequence of brutal intervention by the Turkish authorities, about half a million Kurds have been driven from their homes. An approach like this amounts to collective punishment.[3] Tens of thousands of people, including civil servants, teachers, scientists and politicians were dismissed or imprisoned after the attempted putsch in 2016. The death penalty is due to be reintroduced. The Turkish parliament has been stripped of its power, and the powers of the president have been strengthened. These are all signs clearly reminiscent of the Nazi dictatorship, under which Brunhilde Pomsel began her career in the Reich Broadcasting Corporation after it was cleansed of Jews.

What we are observing in Turkey is also happening elsewhere in the world, but we are talking about a country aspiring to membership of a community of democratic values — the European Union. Fear of the refugees who are trying to escape the civil war in Syria to reach Europe is a factor in the fate of the European democracies. European states forced the European Union to strike a deal with Turkey, which has been used by the Erdoğan administration to resist external involvement in Turkish domestic matters. Refugees from the Syrian war zone – human beings – are becoming political pawns. The threat on the part of the Turkish state leadership to reopen the borders to refugees is creating a panic elsewhere in Europe, particularly in Germany, but in almost all European countries the idea of taking in even more refugees is being firmly rejected – partly because of fear of a further rise of right-wing populists. So fear makes us indifferent towards human rights.

The 'ugly German' of history is back in the form of the radical PEGIDA and parts of a radicalised AfD (Alternative für Deutschland). People with an immigrant background watch the rise of parties such as AfD with growing concern, and wonder how safe they are in Germany. They are worried about whether attacks by the terrorist regime of the so-called Islamic State will turn the national mood against all immigrants, as the right-wing populists use every means at their disposal to gain ground.

Democracy is the constant attempt to safeguard and protect the rights of the individual. The new right-wing populists, should they come to power, will deny individuals these rights again, and the old anti-fascist warning 'Resist the beginnings' is being uttered far too late. When the chair of AfD, Frauke Petry, posited the possibility of using firearms against refugees – against people fleeing from one of the worst civil wars of the modern age and from failed African states – it portrayed them as fair game. With slogans spreading like wildfire on the internet, more and more people are seeing refugees as bogey-men, and the process of brutalisation continues.

Austria saw a presidential candidate, Norbert Hofer, from the right-wing populist Freedom Party of Austria (FPÖ), threaten on several occasions to dissolve the government and hold new elections in the event of his victory – with the aim of bringing the right-wing populist FPÖ head, Heinz-Christian Strache, to power as chancellor. Even though Hofer's opponent, Alexander Van der Bellen, managed to mobilise enough electors to prevent a right-wing populist victory, the election result (53.8 per cent for Van der Bellen versus 46.2 per cent for Norbert Hofer) was close enough to be extremely alarming, rather than a sigh of relief. Just under half of the Austrian population voted for a right-wing populist who tried to canvass votes with the slogan 'Austria first' and the expression of xenophobic sentiments – and effectively with only two campaign themes: the battle against the old establishment and smear campaigns against refugees.

In large parts of Europe refugees are isolated in mass accommodation with no personal dignity, or, as in Hungary, fought at the border by police and soldiers with tear gas and truncheons. As well as over 400,000 deaths in the Syrian civil war so far, the number of people who die trying to escape to Europe from war and misery is rising daily. This also includes the refugees from African states. The number of dead and missing refugees in the Mediterranean was about 23,000 in the period between 2000 and 2014 alone.[4] The monthly newspaper *Le Monde diplomatique* gives the figure as 23,258.[5] But it wasn't only the sea that proved to be a potential deathtrap – hundreds died of hunger or thirst, cold or hypothermia, or suffocated in trucks or were killed when crossing minefields. According to UNHCR estimates, between 2014 and 2016 another 10,000 people drowned while escaping to Europe, and there is no end in sight to these statistics.[6] The refugee situation is one on which Brunhilde Pomsel gives her own view, taking into account her own experience:

> The indifference of people, which you see over and over again. That we are really in a position to see on television how this terrible story is playing out in Syria, hundreds of people drowning, and then there's a variety show. We don't change our lives because of it. I think that's just how it is in life. Everything is all mixed up.

If we pick out key statements and events from Pomsel's biography, we will have a clearer sense of why the behaviour of each individual will be of central importance for the further development and fate of the Western democracies. In European countries, the majority can still set the tone: 'Liberty, equality, fraternity' – the demands of the French Revolution – are also the basis of the European democracies, but their continued existence is by no means certain. If, during times when it is important to stand up for these democratic values, people remain silent and passive and switch over to a 'variety show', a radical minority will go on defining political daily life with slogans, hatred and harassment of everyone who doesn't fit with their view of the world. They will go on poisoning the political climate, win more and more support by spreading lies and hatred and possibly, in the end, come to power. There is a danger that with our indifference and passivity we will manoeuvre ourselves into a moral debacle in which shocking events become routine and concern for our own safety means that refugees and their fates will be objectified, stigmatised and in the end dehumanised; and all the humanism that has been built up in Europe in the seventy years since the Second World War will be lost in the search for a simple solution.

Turkey's threatened collapse back into dictatorship, Brexit – the departure of the United Kingdom, the second biggest economy, from the European Union – the governmental crisis in Italy, the break with democratic principles and the rule of law in Hungary and Poland, the election successes of the AfD in Germany and the narrowly prevented victory of the FPÖ in Austria as well as the feared successes of the right-wing populists Marine Le Pen in France and Geert Wilders in the Netherlands, are, taken all together, the greatest challenge to the preservation of lasting peace in Europe. This is because the declared aim of the right-wing populists is the end of European integration and a return to nation states.

If a party such as the AfD gets over 20 per cent of votes in the German state of Saxony-Anhalt in March 2016, this percentage offers the potential for a right-wing revolution, even if part of that number is an unthinking protest vote – that is precisely where the danger lies. The rapid rise of the AfD recalls the speed with which the NSDAP worked its way up in the Weimar Republic. First they had 18 per cent, then 30 – and with the election victory in 1933 democracy was over. No one should be so naive as to assume that the AfD will find no more followers after a certain point, or that it is out of the question that the FPÖ will have the Austrian chancellorship within the foreseeable future. Across the whole of Europe we are seeing democracies becoming unstable, and this also applies to the previous gatekeeper of democratic principles – the United States.

The Republican presidential candidate Donald Trump was elected President after he identified Muslims, Latinos and other minorities, as well as the 'old' establishment in Washington, to be responsible for the decline of the American dream, explicitly that of the white middle class. After Trump's election victory, Richard Spencer, figurehead of the ultra-right-wing alt-right movement, called for his supporters to 'party like it's 1933' – the year Hitler came to power.[7]

The Trump movement feeds not only on fury against migrants or refugees, but also on rage against the Democratic establishment. Donald Trump, with his slogan 'Make America Great Again!' brought a broad range of aggrieved Americans into the election booth with racist slogans against Muslims, Mexicans and Latinos that are no different from the slogans that European right-wing populists use. Why shouldn't that work equally well in the United States, Donald Trump may have thought. During the caucuses he exploited the frustration of white workers and the white middle class with sexist and racist slogans to ensure votes for himself. The disparagement of whole population groups was suddenly acceptable, since this was no longer a social-class struggle, but a cultural struggle, in which the white population sought to resist the achievements of the liberal age. The integration of foreigners as well as the rights of women and homosexuals – everything suddenly was and remains up for discussion. This is effectively the dissolution of solidarity.

Brunhilde Pomsel's memory of Joseph Goebbels and his speeches, as well as the reactions of the whipped-up masses, allow us to observe one certainty: the seduction of a people by demagogues with simple and radical solutions works now just as it did back then. The fact that Pomsel only slowly discovered who she was actually serving correlates with her self-confessed naivety, which brought her to the Reich Broadcasting Corporation and later to the Ministry of Propaganda.

> I discovered his true nature only very slowly. I remember the famous event at the Sportpalast – 'Do you want total war?'
>
> [...]
>
> it was really an outburst – like an outburst in a mental hospital, I would say. It was as if held said: now you can all do whatever you want. And then, as if every individual in that crowd had been stung by a wasp, all of a sudden every-one let themselves go, shouting and stamping and wishing they could tear their arms out. The noise was unbearable.
>
> My colleague stood there with her hands clenched; we were both so horrified by what was happening. Not by Goebbels, not just by the people – but by the fact that it was even possible. The two of us weren't part of this crowd. We were onlookers; we were perhaps the only onlookers.
>
> [...]

That one person was capable of putting hundreds of people in a state where they were shouting, shouting, shouting: 'Yes, we want total war!' If you tell somebody that today, they would just shake their head and say, 'Right – were they all drunk or what? What was it that made those people shout like that?'

[...]

At that moment I found him terrible. Frightening. But then I repressed it again.

American participants describe the overheated and aggressive atmosphere at appearances by Donald Trump during his election campaign in similar terms. But his excesses, as conveyed by the world's media, have met with surprisingly little rage in the country that once exported its model of liberal democracy to the European post-war world; as if no one wanted to imagine that Trump, who had been dismissed as a political clown, could make it to the Oval Office. It's not impossible that his victory surprised even Trump himself in the end – and we cannot rule out the possibility of similar surprises in the same vein.

In his tightly scripted victory speech Trump said that he had led a 'movement' on the way to the presidency. By saying this, he was suggesting subliminally that he essentially refused to acknowledge the democratic institutions. The reference to a movement among the people has been a concept often used by authoritarian leaders to escape the control of democratic authorities. 'Only incorrigible inhabitants of cloud-cuckooland can seriously believe that now, in possession of such great power, he will allow those powers who were unable to prevent him from marching all the way to the White House to put the thumb-screws on him,' Richard Herzinger warned in *Die Welt*.[8] Even if, because of the system of checks and balances in the American constitution, Trump presents himself in a more moderate light than he said he would, he has contaminated the political climate in his country for years if not decades. The losers of the American dream were in search of a scapegoat, and Donald Trump has given them that scapegoat. In his view, Muslims, Latin Americans and the Chinese – in fact migrants in general – are responsible for leaving the white middle class behind, and taking their jobs. Next in line for condemnation is globalisation. America has for the first time a president whose declaration of war on the democratic establishment has an extraordinary effect on right-wing populists in Europe, because they sense a chance to do the same, and eventually to introduce a return to nationalism.

The political scientist Albrecht von Lucke has summed up Trump's notions of democracy. Trump's friend–enemy ideology, his emphasis on internal politics and rejection of the international stage has led him to the most serious problem that also explains the jubilation on the part of European populists. 'Trump might only become the spearhead of a new form of democracy that no longer sees itself in a pluralist and diverse sense, but ethnically homogeneous. Victor Orbán has also gauged the actual dimension of the election in his own terms, when he invented a victory of "true democracy". What appears here is a different form of democracy, without a constitutional state and without an opposition.'[9] Von Lucke fears that in these democracies the will of the people is being realised by a charismatic leader, entirely in the spirit of the old Nazi motto: 'One people, one Reich, one Führer.'

In Europe this development has fallen on fertile ground. The current campaign by right-wing populists in the Western world is successful because they can fight for and win over the socially 'left-behind', while the bourgeois middle class slumbers like Sleeping Beauty, unable to interpret the dangers of a fragmented society that has lost its solidarity. Anxiety and ignorance seem to be responsible for the fact that the number of drowned refugees leaves us cold and makes us close borders and watch as the hatred of the right takes effect. These events appear to herald a rerun of the darkest period in humanity's history.

The political indifference that Brunhilde Pomsel describes in the milieu that shaped her in the smart district of Berlin-Südende can also be found today among the predominantly helpful Germans. They reacted without particular protest to the demonstrations of the PEGIDA movement, which, at the peak of its popularity, as in a rally in Dresden, the Turkish-German speaker Akif Pirinçci stirred up the population in a spirit of hatred and the human dignity of Moslems was publicly insulted.

It was perhaps only when Brunhilde Pomsel missed her Jewish neighbour Rosa Lehmann Oppenheimer's soap that she became aware of what was going on around her. When her Jewish friend Eva Löwenthal disappeared in 1943, Brunhilde Pomsel could have known that Jews weren't simply being resettled in the east and that concentration camps were not merely being used to 're-educate' people who were critical of the regime, as propaganda wanted to make people believe according to her account. But she didn't know. Pomsel should interest us because she draws our attention to something: ourselves, our anxieties, our arrogance and our disdain for a freedom that has been fought for in a difficult and bloody struggle – and a misunderstanding of how unity breaks down and brutalisation occurs in times of globalisation.

Until Hitler's seizure of power no one in the Pomsel family was prejudiced against the Jews. Pomsel describes her circle of friends at the age of twenty-two as an apolitical 'clique' of spoilt boys. One has an image in front of one's eyes: the boys in white shirts, with braces or in jackets, in heavy leather shoes, their hair combed neatly to the side, gathering with the girls in their fashionable dresses. All a bit more elegant than the average Berliner. A motorbike was a sensation; the beer shared in the pub was a compensation and escape in a time of economic decline and political upheaval. Only very few people had a telephone, only adults read the newspapers, radio and television were still in the developmental stage, the modern age was still only just beginning, and politics was completely uninteresting to the 'clique'. There were no Jews in their circle of friends; her close friend Eva Löwenthal was an exception.

Before 1933 nobody thought about the Jews anyway; it was all invented by the Nazis later on. It was only National Socialism that made us aware that they were different people. Later that was all part of the planned programme for the extermination of the Jews. We had nothing against

Jews. On the contrary: my father was very glad to have some Jewish customers, because they had the most money and always paid well. We played with the children of the Jews. There was one girl, Hilde – she was nice. And next door I remember a Jewish child my age, and I played with him sometimes, and then there was our Rosa Lehmann Oppenheimer; I remember her too. So it never occurred to us that there was anything wrong with them. When we were growing up, nothing at all. And when National Socialism came closer and closer, we still didn't understand what might come. And we waved at our beloved Führer. And why not? First people wanted work and money. We had lost everything in the war, and the Versailles Treaty defrauded us, we were later taught.

None of us had any idea what was coming our way with Hitler.

If Brunhilde Pomsel claims not to have understood in advance what Adolf Hitler's seizure of power would mean, today, in the age of the mass media and the internet, that is no longer possible – or barely – in any Western society. Every negative spin, almost every speech, every new bit of taboo-busting by the right-wing populists goes globally 'viral' on the internet, is passed on unquestioningly on social networks and is permanently stored. It has been proven for a long time that Facebook and other platforms have become the central medium for radicalisation and mobilisation. Even so, Facebook denies any responsibility for the distribution of hate posts and propaganda. Independent of any truth content, the Facebook algorithm provides everything the radical heart could crave, reinforcing prejudices and confirming the user's existing worldview. The internet is becoming a medium for spewing out hatred, since the elements of discontent can come together more easily than before.

Right-wing populists understand that they can reach a big public on the internet without journalists, using an old strategy like the one used by the National Socialists, namely defaming the press as 'the lying press' – a concept that Joseph Goebbels used to denounce his critics. Conversely, right-wing populists in the present day are aiming for a de-rationalisation of reality. 'Post-truth', the word of the year in 2016, is a term for the strategy of right-wing populists to gain support by spreading lies and whipping up hysteria.

Donald Trump's election campaign would have been much less successful without the defamation of the press and the distribution of the supposed truth via social media, whose networks provide a refuge in which users can uninhibit-edly exchange thoughts and information with like-minded people.[10] The right-wing populists know how to make unre-strained use of mistrust for the purposes of agitation. The conspiracy theories surrounding the consequences of the financial crisis as well as the fear of globalisation and grow-ing numbers of refugees are employed to seduce people who feel that their situation is precarious. Young people tend not to use conventional sources for information: a study of 90,000 Austrians reached the shattering conclusion that 85 per cent of those aged between eighteen and thirty-five distrust the traditional media.[11] No less impressive is a study carried out for the *Trust Barometer*: between 2015 and 2016 the global PR agency Edelman questioned over 30,000 people from a total of twenty-eight countries around the world about their trust in elites, and in more than half of countries in Europe the general public's trust in politics, the economy and not least the media has fallen to a level below 50 per cent.[12]

In Europe a justified concern is growing that the spread of fake reports and lies on the internet could massively influence elections, a topic much discussed after the election of the 45th US president. Quite rightly too, because Trump's advocates, including the online magazine *Breitbart News Network*, which has been described as racist, have spread fake reports over the internet that stir up feelings against Muslims and other minorities. *Breitbart* also reported all kinds of rumours about presidential candidate Hillary Clinton, presenting them as facts. Clinton was not only attacked because of the email scandal and was described as a money-grubbing puppet of Wall Street but, in spite of accusations that were refuted long ago, she was also held responsible for the attack on the American consulate in Benghazi in Libya on 11 September 2012. In addition, there were rumours of a new sex scandal involving her husband, Bill Clinton, even though no proof was provided.

In Germany too, media outlets such as *Compact* magazine very successfully spread crude conspiracy theories, which are in every respect a match for Trump's. *Compact* speaks of the deliberate *Umvolkung* – ethnic cleansing – of the German people by migrants; democratically legitimate parties are defamed as 'traitors to the people'; or unexamined news items are put out about rapes that are supposed to have been committed by refugees – these are later revealed as lies, but can still spread their power like wildfire. Nothing is sacred to right-wing populists, and as in the United States the strategy of rabble-rousing and fake reports can bear fruit because what Joseph Goebbels could 'only' circulate via radio and film can acquire much greater power on the internet.

Brunhilde Pomsel remembers in her own way the beginning of escalating rabble-rousing, which would later lead to the mass murder of the Jews.

But how, what, why? We didn't know. Until that terrible business in November 1938 – the night of the Reich pogrom.

We were all shocked that such a thing could happen. That they should have beaten up Jewish people, people of any kind, and that they had broken the windows of Jewish shops and taken things out. In all parts of the city. Well yes, that's where it really began. We were shaken awake. And then somebody, a friend or relative, said that somewhere neighbours had been taken away by people in uniform. They collected them and drove them away in trucks. Where to? No one knew. Of course that was shocking for everyone who had never paid much attention to politics, and that included us... terrible.

Is our present-day passive horror enough to resist the creeping radicalisation of parts of the population against minorities? The terrible events described by Brunhilde Pomsel, which were impossible to resist in those days because the dictatorship was in complete control of everything, had been preceded by a slow process of agitation. The Nazis also started with defamation and propaganda against the Jews, before anti-Jewish laws were introduced after the seizure of power, and in the end there was open persecution after the state-ordained Reich pogrom night, which encountered no resistance from the German population.

In 2016 Donald Trump's populist rhetoric actually revives memories of the darkest times, because the mechanisms and effects of stirred-up hatred are the same as during the rise of the Nazi dictatorship. If the number of attacks on Muslims rose briefly at first after the assault on the World Trade Center on 11 September 2001, the authorities were able to identify a subsequent fall-off in such incidents. Even before Donald Trump's election victory it was feared that the number of crimes committed against minorities and particularly against Muslims would rise again. In fact the number of hate crimes in the United States leapt after election day, 8 November 2016. The Southern Poverty Law Center recorded over 900 reports of harassment and possible hate crimes immediately after Trump's election.[13]

A mixture of fear, passivity and ignorance about right-wing populists also left the people of Britain shocked once they became aware of the consequences of Brexit, and the number of criminal attacks on foreigners multiplied the day after the referendum. Only a few days after the British voted to leave the European Union, the Metropolitan Police provided figures that demonstrate a direct correlation with pre-Brexit propaganda, primarily directed against eastern European immigrants. In

London alone, between the vote on 23 June and the end of July 2016, there were over 2,000 racially motivated attacks.[14] While Polish citizens in the UK were themselves affected by racism, on 11 November 2015 far-right organisations had demonstrated in Poland against Warsaw's proposal to take in refugees, chanting 'Poland for the Poles!' Participants in the march were not only typical nationalists, but also people who had been assumed to belong to the political centre.[15]

In Germany a wave of xenophobia assumed dramatic form as long ago as the 1990s, with fatal attacks on asylum-seekers' refuges. These included the sieges of hostels in Hoyerswerda in 1991 and Rostock-Lichtenhagen in 1992, as well as the deadly attacks on families of Turkish origin in Mölln in 1993 and Solingen in 1996, in which a total of eight people lost their lives. Since the refugee crisis the mood in Germany has worsened. The Amadeu Antonio Foundation and PRO ASYL, in a chronicle that covered only the year 2015, registered 1,072 attacks on refugee hostels, including 136 arson attacks. A total of 267 people were injured. The rise in these incidents is particularly concerning against the background of the rise of the AfD, which with its xenophobic slogans and a direct connection with the PEGIDA movement helped right-wing acts of violence achieve record levels. The figure for these attacks in 2016 was more than 44 per cent higher than the previous year. These are exclusively attacks in which people are harmed or could have lost their lives when stones and firebombs are thrown at their hostels, or they are attacked with pistols and explosives. But in comparison to the 1990s, there are very few counter-protests against these attacks.

Under the Nazi dictatorship, Brunhilde Pomsel's only possible response to the developments was to take horrified note of them. But what about us now? In the 1990s, after the attacks in Mölln and Solingen, for weeks at a time concerts and candlelit demonstrations showed a country that refused to accept this form of prejudice. In Frankfurt alone, in December 1992, 150,000 people took part in a concert with the motto 'Heute die! Morgen du!' (Them today, you tomorrow). In Munich on 6 December 1992 more than 400,000 people took to the streets and formed a candlelit procession against xenophobia and the far right.[16]

And today? Is the cosy lethargy of the moderate bourgeoisie not partly responsible for the fact that in 2016 the German Federal Criminal Office anxiously expects further serious right-wing acts of violence? In regard to the new bogeyman of the 'refugee', the otherwise very divided far-right movement seems to have reached a far greater consensus than that achieved by what we may still assume to be the overwhelming majority of people attached to the democratic structure. Can a society with democratic principles afford to allow opponents of a new home for asylum seekers in Clausnitz in Central Saxony to block the provision of accommodation for refugees? The pictures have been seen on the internet, all over the world: about 100 demonstrators blocking a bus full of refugees as it attempted to reach a hostel and chanting 'We are the people!' They prevented the passengers from leaving the bus, so that the frightened refugees from war zones could only be brought to safety with the help of the police. Can we afford to wait until, like Joseph Goebbels's secretary, we only watch the terrible events in silent horror before getting on with the business of the day?

If we think about Hitler and the Third Reich, the Holocaust is presumably still the greatest act of barbarism of all time. But the history of National Socialism began long before that. The first attempted putsch was in 1923, and the Nazi façade and ideology were built up step by step. Even if, in her safe little world, Brunhilde Pomsel showed no interest in the political development of her country, it was still insidiously taking place. Anyone who dares to make comparisons with the present day is not relativising Nazism. It is not a comparison in the sense of a one-to-one match, it is a matter of recognising signs of the danger of new radical trends in the present – and those signs, taken all together, are grave enough. Right-wing populists are once again awakening the lowest instincts in the population, by portraying particular groups of people as inferiors. In the end, people hate other people as a way of feeling better about themselves, in the absence of any sense of self-worth. Contempt and hatred become collective self-empowerment. The willingness of populists to resort quite openly to racist rhetoric, or to threaten their political opponents with their removal, can be shown with reference to their inflammatory speeches.

In December 2015, Donald Trump, to thunderous applause from his supporters, advocated a travel ban for Muslims and, a short time later, racial profiling: that is, action by the police against people who are held to be suspicious on the basis of their skin colour, religion, nationality or ethnic origin, and the possibility of arrest on those grounds.[17]

In October 2016, the parliamentary party leader of the AfD, Björn Höcke, called for the removal of 'elites': 'We have a completely exhausted old elite, as I call it. We don't just have old parties, we have old media, we have an old elite. Some things will need to be cleared away in this country, and this old elite is so exhausted that it has to go. We will have to dispose of that old elite.'[18] His exhortation fatally recalls a speech given by Joseph Goebbels in July 1932, a good six months before the Nazi seizure of power, in a radio broadcast: 'We do not need to negotiate with parties and systems hostile to us except in so far as we want to remove them.'[19] Less than a year later the National Socialists came to power and began removing their political opponents.

In January 2017, to frantic cheers from his supporters, Höcke upped the ante, when he referred among other things to the Holocaust Memorial in Berlin: 'We Germans, our people, are the only people in the world that has planted a monument of shame in the heart of its capital.'[20] He was not only kicking out at the memory of the six million murdered Jews and those from other marginalised groups, but was relativising the most serious crime against humanity in history.

In September 2015 Marine Le Pen used the refugee policy of the German Chancellor Angela Merkel to consolidate her ambitions for the French presidency. In a speech in Brussels she declared that the sovereignty of the EU countries was 'threatened by an enemy [...] who is working and plotting only a few streets away from here'. She meant the 'Euro-dictatorship of the European Commission'. The Commission, she argued, was trying to conceal its true nature: 'a machine for crushing peoples, a sower of austerity [...] and now a receptionist for all the illegals on the planet'.[21]

If one is inclined, on the basis of Brunhilde Pomsel's biography, to condemn her, the question naturally arises whether our behaviour in the present day is so very different from that of the people in the Third Reich. Have we not reached a much more dramatic form of ignorance and apathy if such inflammatory speeches have no consequences, even though we know where they can lead? Unlike the generation that saw Adolf Hitler or Benito Mussolini as the salvation from economic misery, or at least tacitly agreed when they assumed power, because of our knowledge of history we are aware of the consequences of such a dictatorship. In her reflections, however, Pomsel sees today's youth as far less ignorant and naive.

> Politics was largely uninteresting as far as we were concerned. When I see what schoolgirls get up to today, expressing their opinions and everything, I think to myself: my God, that's a difference; that's an incredible difference. Then I sometimes think: I'm not over a hundred years old, I'm three hundred years old. Their whole way of life is completely different.

But in a 2016 survey not even a fifth of all German and Austrian young people said they were interested in politics at all.[22] Today's young people are not the first generation to have grown up largely apolitical. The same applies to 'Generation Y', born between 1980 and the turn of the millennium. Former Daimler CEO Edzard Reuter insists that that generation is completely unprepared for the crises of the present as they have never been interested in politics, and even holds them responsible for the rise of the populists, who have had an easy ride since all they had to do was construct threatening scenarios whose contents were never examined. The generation of 1968 got a lot of things wrong, but they always argued, got engaged and involved. The former head of Daimler doesn't say this without putting some of the responsibility on the democratic elites. Political debate is an indispensable element of any democracy. Controversies are only staged for the next round of elections, while genuine problems aren't addressed. 'No wonder young people don't think anyone's telling them the truth.'[23]

According to a survey by the University of Konstanz,[24] fewer and fewer students in Germany are taking an interest in politics. If we look closely at the opinion polls we can identify a trend towards political apathy and passivity. A majority of respondents are chiefly concerned about their own future and career. They hope that their studies will give them not only good training, but also an interesting job as well as a decent income. These findings are very similar to those of the 17th Shell Youth Study,[25] which shows that most young people are primarily concerned about their individual happiness and a materially secure future, and barely take any interest in politics and the common good.

In the United States the figures don't look very different. In September 2008, 65 per cent of eighteen- to twenty-nine-year-olds said they took an interest in elections, and by September 2012 this had fallen to 48 per cent. And while in

2008 72 per cent claimed they had decided to vote, this had declined in 2012 to 63 per cent.[26]

The political indifference of the younger generation is also apparent from the referendum on the departure of the UK from the European Union. Young Britons who were eligible to vote on 23 June 2016 – but didn't – admitted with horror that they hadn't expected the result. They had simply assumed that those in favour of remaining in the EU would win in any case. The fact that they complained the following day about the loss of the advantages of being in the EU is a direct consequence of political indifference, because they could have influenced the result in their favour by making use of their right to vote.

For a large proportion of the younger generation, the need for self-expression is at the centre of everyday activity. The perfect stage for that is the internet, with its platforms like Facebook, Instagram and Twitter to satisfy their hunger for self-promotion; something once done only by those in the colourful pages of glossy magazines is now imitated by millions of young people on the internet. However, anyone who criticises the younger generation, as Edzard Reuter has, mustn't ignore the fact that the young face all kinds of insecurities. Their relationship with the world of work is increasingly precarious, and since 9/11 they have been confronted with the threat of terrorism like no other generation since the Second World War. Yet in two respects they are distinctly at an advantage compared to the youth of the 1930s: they have had a far better education; and they have grown up with the concept of universal human rights.[27]

But it is also true that in spite of their education, many of the young barely have a chance of genuine participation. In Europe this applies particularly to countries such as Greece, Spain or Portugal – where, since the financial crisis of 2008 and the subsequent euro crisis, youth unemployment has hit record levels – and also parts of East Germany. It is beyond dispute that many of the young in Europe and the United States have no positive expectations of the future. 'They are the first generation since the Second World War that fears that they won't be able to achieve or maintain the standard of living and the quality of life enjoyed by their parents,' says the sociologist Zygmunt Bauman.[28] This produces anger and hatred on one hand, and on the other a lack of interest in politics as well as resignation at not being able to improve their own situation through political engagement. Even if many young people seem different today – modern, networked and well educated – a good number are as apolitical, resigned or indifferent as Brunhilde Pomsel in her day, and just as preoccupied with themselves as the 'clique' she describes.

The young in Western democracies after 9/11 did not grow up in authoritarian conditions, but they did grow up with uncertainty and insecurity. Knowing the history of the twentieth century, their interest should be in the preservation of democracy. And to do that, online petitions will hardly be enough. Great waves of rage on the internet have no consequences for society, because this kind of protest has few political or social consequences – although the same cannot be said of rabble-rousing by demagogues. A statement in favour of an environmental protection project or against intensive farming leads to no obligations of any kind for its signatories. Activities such as online petitions fit with the general image of this generation – involving only fleeting involvement – and are essentially no different from hedonistic consumerism. 'All too often it looks as if political activity is little more than a refined form of consumerism, which is chiefly popular with the affluent who can present their identity relatively simply, and show what a good cause they have chosen',[29] as the British political scientist Gerry Stoker observes in his book *Why Politics Matters*. The condemnation inherent in this statement should perhaps be viewed with scepticism, but its negative effect may be relevant for the maintenance of a democratic order.

The problem of every analysis of a generation is that it is conducted with the aspirations and value judgements of an earlier generation. From this point of view, Brunhilde Pomsel views the contemporary situation of young people in comparison with her own time, and confuses the present generation's technical advances and greater access to knowledge with greater interest and political activity.

We were stupid in those days. There wasn't time to think about everything – ordinary people would be thinking about when they had to go to work. In my circle we were largely untouched by problems. They didn't burden or preoccupy us, the way they preoccupy me now that my life is behind me. I'm much more interested in them now. I'm just trying to explain to you how as a young person who is simply released into life there seems to be some kind of direction. But it doesn't always need to be an influence. That's easier to observe in the present day.

In Europe, the possibility of an active peace movement among the younger generation, of the kind seen in the days of the nuclear threat between East and West, is very remote. In spite of a precarious labour market, a rise in far-right activism in the streets, mass attacks on refugees, and terrible civil wars like the one being waged in Syria, large numbers of the younger generation seem resigned or indifferent. Brunhilde Pomsel also did not reflect upon the political situation of her time, and even today she doesn't think much of the speeches delivered by the politicians.

If I had been able to guess or know everything back then, I certainly wouldn't have gone to the Broadcasting Corporation or the Propaganda Ministry. For me, Goebbels was a politician who tended to shout a bit loudly. I didn't think about it at all. I also never listened to all that codswallop, his speeches. Everyone was saying the same things. I don't listen to speeches in the Bundestag either. It's all just claptrap, what they come out with.

We might be inclined to judge Pomsel's opinion about the speeches in the Bundestag against the background of her experiences — and yet she speaks for a majority of the population. Her perception doesn't just demonstrate resignation towards the present on the part of the older generation, but shows a form of turning away from politics that had been summed up since the 1980s in the term 'political fatigue' (*Politikverdrossenheit*). This became the word of the year in Germany as early as 1992, and shows another form of ignorance and indifference on the part of the political elite itself, because the voters' clearly observed disenchantment with politics did not lead to a change in the actions of politicians. For almost three decades this detachment from mainstream politics was ignored by the Western elites, and this has now became a dangerous mixture of radicalisation on the one hand and ignorance and political indifference on the other. Far-right attitudes didn't suddenly appear in society, but had been anchored there for a long time, and the only question is what proportion of the population really holds far-right views, since the success of the right can also be explained with reference to a vague mood of protest among the discontented and anxious. They are primarily concerned with giving a sign, a warning to the elites, without supporting the radical demands of the populists. Dangerously, however, they don't question them either. The fury and humiliation have reached a point where facts no longer count.[30] Before we examine whether the democratic elites have themselves failed the voters out of ignorance and indifference, we should examine the socio-economic parallels with the 1930s.

In the 1930s the situation — in terms of material conditions, as well as the unemployment of large numbers of the population — was far more dramatic after the stock market crash of 1929 than it is today. The 2008 crash did not have such devastating effects, yet it created the greatest economic crisis and the worst recession since 1930, and there are fears that the effects of the 2008 financial crisis are still ahead of us in the form of mass unemployment and large-scale social decline. So far it has been possible to mitigate the impact of the financial crash and the crisis in the euro, but people sense that it could get worse at any time. Today, in parts of the population, even the *fear* of possible social decline as in the 1930s seems to be so powerful that the urge to survive emerges at the expense of social minorities – a fatal reflex that shows how torn society is. This is directly connected with the development of global-isation and the economic system that underpins it.

Among those who voted for the new right-wing populists there are some who feel overtaxed by the globalised world, even when they have so far suffered no material disadvantages from it, and yet they despise open borders and the 'old elites' who are untroubled by their concerns. People feel alienated and powerless, according to many analyses by the Western media. The excess of information, which is now digitally avail-able to everyone, intensifies the perception of an excessively complex world and the longing for simple answers. The new bogeymen are the migrants; they too want some security and material comfort, but the protest voters are worried that they themselves will lose out as a result.

Such anxieties, and subjective emotions, often ignored, may be described as follows: if in Germany a mother of three children, who has spent her whole life working, feels that she will eventually be reliant on welfare, a problem arises – the feeling of humiliation. When an employee reaches the income level of a refugee, even though he may have paid into the social welfare system for twenty or thirty years, for many that is an unspeakable injustice. The fact that there may be good reasons why refugees receive state support seems irrelevant to them; they feel only that they are being treated unjustly and their own way of life is under threat.

The cause for the lack of interest in facts in favour of a 'perceived truth' — the socio-political process that was described in 2016 as 'post-truth' — lies in wounded feelings, expectations and incomprehension in the face of an unjust world. But in the end it may have less to do with 'factual poverty' than with 'perceived poverty', which in sociological terms is a complex phenomenon, since the feeling depends not only on socio-economic conditions but also on the personal environment of social experiences, social position and in the end of world view. The feeling of injustice seems to encourage a search for a scapegoat and a longing for simple answers. Even Brunhilde Pomsel refers to the humiliation that the Germans felt in the face of defeat in the First World War, which made it so easy for Hitler.

Is today's world still not comparable with the 1930s? Then as now, the collapse did not occur from one day to the next. Misery and rage grew slowly. In the everyday experience of the economic crisis certain social classes could still live in a relatively carefree way, and what Brunhilde Pomsel describes for the Berlin of the 1930s also applies to post-crash Detroit, Athens in the wake of austerity politics or the regions of Germany that face social decline.

But while Berlin might have been praised to the skies, it had always had its dark sides, and particularly then, after losing the First World War. Unemployed people on every corner, beggars, poor people. Anyone who lived in good areas, as I did, in a good suburb, didn't see any of that. Of course there were particular areas swarming with poverty and wretchedness; you didn't want to see things like that, you just looked away.

Looking away runs through Brunhilde Pomsel's biography like a thread – but in that she wasn't and isn't alone. The democratic parties of the Weimar Republic are often blamed for the collapse of democracy, because they lacked the courage to assume responsibility and a willingness to co-operate across party boundaries. The dispute between the parties was more important to them than the solution of the great problems of the time. People in the Germany of the 1930s did not look inwards, so they were ignorant of the real and emotionally felt decline of large parts of the population, and in the end they looked away as the supposed 'enemy of the people' was defined, persecuted, expelled and murdered.

Both then and now, upheaval and radicalisation were preceded by unhampered globalisation. In the 1920s, for many countries, there were no travel restrictions or visa requirements. As in the crash of 1929, speculation on the stock exchange in 2008 had fatal consequences. In both historical situations after the crash there were a few winners and many losers, although in 2008 these were more perceived than real. However, in both historical situations masses of people in Europe and the United States had either lost their jobs and were unable to earn a living or had huge concerns about the future. As in the present day, the forces of global-isation, once unleashed, escaped national state control. The political institutions lost their ability to solve problems and a fatal vacuum was created, since the state was no longer able to fulfil its protective function towards its people, and Brunhilde Pomsel stresses that from then on things were easy for Hitler.

Attempts were made to mitigate the damage done to financial market capitalism in the present day through economic measures, but in spite of the crisis bankers' bonuses contin-ued to rise while the monetary policies of the central banks in Europe and the United States gradually devalued life insur-ance, the purchasing power of pensions and some other forms of public service. The European governments also undertook serious cuts in the welfare state, and labour market reforms made working relations increasingly precarious.

People in the 1930s did not necessarily grasp the complex connections between stock-market speculation and the global economic crisis, while today people are kept informed daily about both inequality and the inactivity of politics. Even today politics seems to be driven by crises rather than exerting control over a given situation; a hazardous vacuum has been created. In her reflection, Brunhilde Pomsel says of the time before Hitler:

> After the end of the First World War Germany was leader-less. There were no personalities there, and that was why it was so easy for Hitler. Too many unemployed, and they were his whole support.

This lack of leadership has also been used by right-wing populists in the present day. For reasons of respect towards the victims of the Second World War the social conflict and poverty in large parts of the population and inaction on the part of politicians cannot be directly compared with the present-day situation. Not yet, anyway.

But by the end of the 1990s the fuse for the renewed scenario of a failure of liberal democracy as the result of an unregulated financial industry had been lit in the United States. Since the presidency of Bill Clinton (1993–2001), the Democrats – the left-wing and liberal forces in the United States – 'New Labour' in the UK and the Social Democrats of Europe had surrendered to the laws of neo-liberal globalisation, when the financial markets were deregulated in spite of urgent warnings from leading economists. In Britain under Tony Blair's government this led to a policy of social indifference and under Gerhard Schröder in Germany to Agenda 2010, with massive cuts to the welfare system, a softening of labour market laws and the weakening of trade unions. The shrinking of the welfare state went hand in hand with an enormous expansion of the financial sector and growth in the low-wage sector. Step by step the left had betrayed a considerable proportion of their voters – working and lower-middle class, some of whom are now being radicalised. What appears more and more clearly is that the ignorance and the inactivity of the democratic elites are responsible for a division in Western societies, and have made it so easy for right-wing populists to gain a foothold.

Albrecht von Lucke writes that: 'Societies are divided into an open liberal metropolitan elite and an increasingly déclassé lower class, whose fears of decline radiate upwards more and more powerfully.'[31] This leads to a feeling of panic, which has now reached the middle class and made racism socially acceptable. Because of the economic decline of whole population groups in the United States and Europe, as in the 1930s, faith in democracy to intervene with regulations has been weakened. More than that, by spreading conspiracy theories, rightwing forces create the suspicion that 'the ones at the top' want to halt the social decline of large sections of the population.

While in Europe, as in the United States, the economic losses were quietly modified by low interest rates and by redirecting tax income to failing banks, the achievements of a social market economy and democracy based on balance and social peace were sacrificed to the neo-liberal market ideology. But contemporary neo-liberalism did not appear overnight, and it exploited people's faith that globalisation would mean an expansion of the social market economy. The opposite occurred, and globalisation became the project of the elite and the super-rich.

In the 1930s too, when Brunhilde Pomsel began her career, the same spiral of national isolationism had been set in motion that Donald Trump announced before his election to the US presidency. Then too, out of concern about European economic migrants, first of all only selected foreigners were allowed into the country. In a similar way Europe's borders are being closed, asylum laws intensified, and the British are about to leave the European Union. In everyday life the misery of masses of people, as described by Brunhilde Pomsel, is ignored both by the state and by the affluent bourgeoisie. The stock market crash of 1929 was followed by a rightward shift almost everywhere in Europe – just as support for nationalists of all colours has been growing constantly since the financial crisis. This is not happening at random; the leaders of the democratic elites are contributing to the loss of their credibility every day.

Revelations about the secret offshore businesses of dozens of heads of state and other wealthy people are regularly published in the media. When the super-rich and large companies take their money to tax havens, without paying taxes like everyone else, the inevitable impression is that globalisation can no longer be controlled for the benefit of the general population. On the contrary, in fact. These hidden fortunes, in the billions, grant a small elite of the super-rich an incredible amount of power, in the face of which all government looks powerless, as the journalist Harald Schumann has observed: 'The entire political class in Europe – including the Greens and even part of the left – has essentially capitulated. They know it is the companies, the banks and the super-rich who decide on the fortunes of their states, regions and municipalities.'[32] The political parties of the Weimar Republic received a similar judgement.

The crisis of democracy is the result, developed over a long period of time, of helpless-looking politicians who saw no alternative to the rescue of the banks after the financial crisis, which was seen as capitulation by both the left and right wings. Many in these groups reject globalisation while the political elite capitulates to the greed of the financial industry, and right-wing populists exploit the fury and despair of the population for their own purposes. In the West, a fragmented society no longer forms a unified community. The sovereignty of the European democratic elites and parties is now vanishing, since they have shown themselves – or at least given the impression – as being incapable of serving the common good.

As in the 1930s the appeal of the populists lies in the promise of supposedly simple solutions. But simple solutions are extremely dangerous, because it is much more difficult to change them than it is to let them come into being. Terrorism, debt crises, climate change, refugees – these problems can no longer be solved at a national level, and yet more and more people are following this reflex of simplification. The moderate middle class of the bourgeoisie seems now, as then, primarily preoccupied with itself.

Personal challenges are now oscillating between family and career, in a flexible labour market. The model follows that of the American dream, which since the financial crisis has been revealed as a nightmare: everyone is responsible for himself, the social network becomes ever more fragmented, and the overriding emotion is not freedom but insecurity. What still seemed certain to the generation of 'baby boomers', that they could work their way up through their own efforts, is no longer valid, either in the United States or in Europe. The advantages of Western capitalism have become so fragile that many people are questioning the purpose of a democracy in which companies and the wealthy are so much better off than individual citizens. Here populists on both left and right find many ways of breaking down social cohesion. What has long been heralded is now becoming reality: the people promising salvation have reappeared. As Brunhilde Pomsel remembers the period immediately after Hitler's rise to power:

> But immediately after Hitler's accession, the mood was simply one of new hope. It was still a huge surprise that Hitler had done it. I think they were surprised themselves.

Are Western societies today, out of egoism on the one hand and ignorance and indifference towards the populists on the other, stumbling blindly into a new nightmare?

One other mobilising factor is the indifference, even mockery, from the liberal-democratic elites towards the groups voting for right-wing parties, which hardly contributes to a solution. Elisabeth Raether explains in a remarkable essay in *Die Zeit* that with their arrogance the liberal elites have themselves become part of the crisis, while the so-called 'left-behind' voting classes want to take their revenge on 'the ones at the top'.[33] Those groups of the population with college degrees and a more or less secure job despise those without these advantages for not being so tolerant towards immigrants and other minorities. But on the other hand, graduate jobs are not potentially threatened by immigrants, and employed graduates are not afraid of competition for social services. The potential losers in globalisation are standing outside our labour exchanges, just as the refugees stand outside our borders. The refugees and right-wing populists should remind us that our efforts to achieve a better world are failing before our eyes.

Part of the task of democratic parties is to take the fury of the voters and uncomfortable truths seriously when they are delivered, for example in the form of survey results that reflect the mood in the population. When researchers at the University of Leipzig established in 2016, for example, that half of all Germans sometimes feel like foreigners in their own country because of the many Muslims living there, and 41 per cent think Muslims should be banned from coming to Germany from the outset, this refers to a part of the population much larger as a percentage than those who have so far voted for the right-wing AfD. To deny or repress this insecurity and discontent in the population is much more dangerous than to conduct a public debate about a general limitation on immigration. If such opinions become deeply rooted and in the end half of the population refuses further migration, one cannot simply dismiss them out of hand. If bourgeois forces do not face the fear and potential radicalisation of a population, and if governments do not invest in combating the reasons for refugees fleeing to other countries in the first place, then they should be honest and get to the heart of the price of isolationism: infringement of human rights, international law and militarised border facilities.

A study by the British opinion poll institute Ipsos MORI shows that the Germans, like almost all other citizens in Europe and the United States, are completely wrong in their assessment of the supposed flood of Muslim migrants. One in five people living in Germany, or 21 per cent of the country's population, is of Muslim faith, the respondents estimated. In fact it is only one in twenty, or 5 per cent of the population as a whole – and that is after the big wave of refugees in 2015. Even today it is not clear how many people will return to Syria after the end of the civil war, which would further reduce the proportion of Muslims in the population. This misapprehension is even clearer in the United States, where the proportion is 1 per cent as against an estimated 17 per cent.[34]

A society can overcome the brutalisation of the modern age only if it has a reliable framework for order outside of nationalist and isolationist policy, and unmasks the populists and their completely unrealistic promises as well as their lies. Only if all democratic forces manage to engage objectively with the facts rather than being guided by emotions can the increase in numbers moving to the right-wing populists be halted. For this to happen, the social problems and dislocations of neo-liberal capitalism, the financial and economic crisis, the parallels with the 1930s set out here, must first be taken seriously.

There could be a good side to the rise of the right-wing populists, because hitherto socio-political issues were not on the agenda of the elites. At the last meeting of the G20 states in September 2016 the governments of the twenty largest industrial nations declared that the advantages of globalisation must be more widely distributed. Perhaps this plan even went into action because the elites feared a return to the 1930s, and if this is the case then there is a chance of reform in globalisation.

Moreover, it is not clear that the moderate bourgeoisie will be content to simply watch the rise of the right-wing populists from afar. There is a chance that the election of Trump, the close election result in Austria, the dismantling of democracy in Poland and Hungary, Brexit and the situation in Turkey and Syria as well as the general brutalisation of Western democracies were a final warning for the elections in France, the Netherlands and Germany. The emphasis is on 'chance', because the enemies of democracy are still storming the parliaments.

Equally, out of sheer fear and ignorance, we are obviously standing under the 'bell jar' described by Brunhilde Pomsel, in which a general obsession with personal advantage, along with opportunism and denial of the current social situation, continue to aid the rise the right-wing populists. Perhaps those who lived through the Nazi regime could plead a lack of knowledge – but we know the course of history, and should know better. It will be a long and difficult battle to repel the right-wing populists and above all to win back their voters for a democratic constitutional state, and for European unity, which will involve engaging with the demands of those groups of voters who are turning away from democracy.

More liberal demands for tolerance and the protection of minorities will not succeed alone; it will also require measures that, after the terrorist attacks in Europe in 2015 and 2016, will create a feeling of security. That refugees must officially register and the state must be in a position to filter out dangerous individuals and other criminals is obvious from a constitutional point of view. But this must be done in spite of the shrill demands for expulsion, isolationism and other repressive measures on the part of the right-wing populists, without endangering the human rights of refugees fleeing civil wars, and migrants in general. We citizens must show moral courage in defending these rights, even in everyday life.

We must not forget that one of the most important lessons from the failed refugee policy of the international community in the 1930s and 1940s concerned the rejection of Jewish refugees, since no worldwide agreement could be reached on taking them in. In 1937, when growing persecution caused a mass flight of the Jewish population, there was barely a country that allowed unlimited immigration. When the Nazi regime at last forbade all emigration in October 1941, it was almost impossible for the Jews who had stayed in the German Reich to flee annihilation. It wasn't until after the Second World War that binding agreements were reached for the protection of refugees, in the form of a treaty that still applies today – the 1951 Geneva Convention on Refugees. It obliges us to never send people in search of protection back to where they are threatened by persecution.

The demand for secure borders and social justice are therefore not demands that a democratic society should leave to right-wing populists – who in any case question the international legal principle of the Geneva Convention – and certainly not when at the core of their mostly simplified analysis there may be a kernel of truth. But neither in the past nor in the present day have right-wing populists of every type even begun to prove that they were in a position to solve problems peacefully, humanely or permanently. Almost without exception, their power has been exerted at the expense of minorities, with chaos, violence, power and oppression. Populists are generally inclined to make completely unrealistic promises. But as soon as they are in power, the discrepancy between claims and reality often becomes apparent. There are plenty of examples from recent history that show that right-wing populist governments generally go in one of two directions: either the interests of the voters are turned into their opposite, or internal disputes lead to the collapse of the party.[35]

Brunhilde Pomsel isn't the only very elderly eyewitness to fascism to have asked whether people have learned from history. The doctor Ingeborg Rapoport, who died at the age of 104, experienced several times what it means to be persecuted: what united her and Brunhilde Pomsel was fear of the new rabble-rousing spirit in Germany in 2016. Ingeborg Rapoport became famous at the age of 102 when she became the oldest person in the world to gain a doctorate. She was born in 1912 in Cameroon – a German colony at the time – grew up in Hamburg and, as a Jew, fled from the Nazis with her mother to the United States. From there, having been denounced as a communist, she had to flee again during the McCarthy era to the GDR, where she later experienced the fall of the Berlin Wall. In an interview, like Brunhilde Pomsel, she describes her own apolitical attitude up to the point when she found herself confronting anti-Semitism in Nazi Germany as a young woman.[36] She remembers an atmosphere of omnipresent fear. The anti-Semitism she would later encounter in the GDR was only latent, but with reunification it came back into the open. The fact that a xenophobic movement like PEGIDA should have established itself in East Germany, of all places, was a great source of concern to her. Every day she listened to the news and took a keen interest in what was happening in the country: the burning of refugee hostels, demonstrators shouting 'Germany for the Germans' and spreading fear – she was familiar with all this, because fear was the most important instrument of the Nazis.

The way people talk about refugees today stirred bad memories in Ingeborg Rapoport. She saw the greatest danger as radicalisation on the one hand and political indifference on the other – 'The apolitical are easy to influence.' The dangerous ones are those who want simple answers to complex questions, she said. She believed in peace-loving people with a sense of solidarity, and not in the ego-driven capitalist system. The derogatory discussion of Islam and the debate around the full-face veil were used, in her view, as a way of stirring up hatred, just like the things she experienced in National Socialism.

In the end, both biographies have one thing in common: Brunhilde Pomsel and Ingeborg Rapoport are perhaps the last warning of a generation that experienced first-hand what fascism, ignorance, passivity and opportunism have done in Germany and the world. The bourgeoisie of the 1920s and 1930s at first despised Adolf Hitler as an idiot and were silent until it was too late. Brunhilde Pomsel, by her own retrospective account, was blind in her quest for success and affluence, and indifferent towards the developments of her time. We too are clearly too lethargic these days to implement the obvious solution: to try to help the disadvantaged in our system have a greater share. Neo-liberalism in its present-day form has sacrificed social solidarity in favour of a narcissistic individuality. Everyone forges his own destiny – not by chance is that saying a symbol of the American dream, which was revealed by the financial crisis of 2008 as creating many, many losers and, in the end, President Donald Trump. Solidarity is the oil in the engine of a democratic, free and humanistic society; if we want to go on putting up with the injustice of an economic system that over the past few years has increasingly fostered disunity to maximise the profits of multinational companies, we are feeding the right-wing populists.

A slow breakdown of solidarity is always followed by dehumanisation. A society in which human instincts such as empathy and solidarity are repressed is such an ugly society that it actually ceases to need democracy. Brunhilde Pomsel's selfish and unreflecting efforts to secure her own advantage are currently taking place a million times over – in ourselves. If democracy bends so deeply to the economy that people think they no longer have any influence on institutions, and even see their interests as being betrayed, then the populists and fascists will have an easy ride over the years to come. The former US Secretary of State Henry Kissinger encapsulates the historical experience in Germany in a single breath: 'We in America must understand that you cannot continually offend the social values of the middle class without eventually being punished for it. Nobody knows this better than Germany.'[37]

A solution will have to be found for migration – or we must assume that tens of thousands of refugees will drown in the Mediterranean or be halted with ever-greater brutality by some European fortress wall and abandoned to their misery. We must begin a discourse on how globalisation can be organised in such a way that the causes for flight can be eliminated, which can only in the end be done through forms of redistribution as well as help in overcoming the effects of climate change and a halt to the exploitation of resources in terms of both people and the environment, and through a peace movement that brings all conflicting parties to the negotiating table. For this to happen we would need something that has generally only existed in the event of world wars – a top-down redistribution, a kind of 'New Deal' for globalisation. The democratic elites must grasp that yet more inequality cannot be in their interests, and must be willing to provide a new impulse: an invitation to participate in democratic decision-making processes that set limits on the excesses of companies and the super-rich, and once again postulate the old maxim as a leitmotif of Western values: that the economy should serve people and not the few super-rich. On his farewell tour of Europe in 2016, the outgoing US President Barack Obama suggested just this change of direction – otherwise a deep-rooted feeling of injustice would continue to prevail.

There isn't much time left to guide globalisation, currently derailed, back on to better and fairer tracks and to remedy the problems in our economic system: plummeting income, the dominance of the banks, the tax evasion of the super-rich and the major companies and the rapid digitisation of the economy, which goes hand in hand with a fear of the loss of jobs in industry as well as our attitude towards democracy and refugees. It is the responsibility of all groups in a society to let everyone participate and to help those who are afraid of an unpredictable future – the disadvantaged in Europe and the United States as well as refugees from further afield.

Drawing historical parallels is always difficult. Still, as I have outlined here, it is possible, and important to remember that the achievements of democracy, for which a lot of blood was shed in Europe, can disappear again. The bourgeoisie, which once watched the rise of Hitler, is also watching the rabble-rousers and radicals. Let us take Brunhilde Pomsel as an example and work to ensure that the right-wing populists do not speak for a silent majority.

We have the fascism of the 1930s as an undeniable blueprint for what Hannah Arendt called 'the banality of evil'. Today we know how the collective mechanism of evil works. There are no more excuses: we know that one participates in evil deeds by the very fact of being unwilling, because of one's own self-centredness, to see what is happening and step in on behalf of the rights and dignity of man. For that reason we are under particular pressure to do this, because we have the benefit of knowing history. Everything else is self-deception. Brunhilde Pomsel's life story should stir us up; it is high time for the moderate middle class to come together and put pressure on the democratic elites to engage in reforms that lead to more justice and solidarity and thus cement the cohesion of Western societies, because the refugee crisis is only the symptom of a global economic order based on competition and disunity.

We can no longer afford to look away, because right-wing demagogues exploit everything they can to damage democracy. The neo-liberal policy of the West bears responsibility for this, and has ensured that the market has become excessively powerful. The social contract that promised social stability has been cancelled. That is why we are living in a time of chance, in which democratic values are being called into question. If the remaining democratic parties and the middle class do not start thinking about how that contract can be revived, we will see a wave of right-wing populism in Europe that will overwhelm democracy in the years to come. It is time for the middle class and the elite in all areas of society to prove that they have learned from history.

ACKNOWLEDGEMENTS

Thanks to the eyewitness Brunhilde Pomsel for her testimony. She made it possible to connect her unusual biography with the threats facing us today. Her memories and contradictions can teach us all a lesson, because freedom and democracy now need our commitment and our full attention.

I would like to thank the film-makers Christian Krönes, Olaf S. Müller, Roland Schrotthofer and Florian Weigensamer for allowing us access to the extensive interviews they had with Brunhilde Pomsel as well as for their close and friendly collaboration. I would also like to thank Gwendolin Hallhuber and Dorothee Boesser for their hard work.

Warm thanks also to the publisher Christian Strasser, who entrusted me with this project in August 2016.

Not least, I am particularly grateful to my editor Ilka Heinemann for her intense co-operation — it was the only way this exciting task could have been performed in such a short time.

Thore D. Hansen
January 2017

NOTES

'WE WEREN'T INTERESTED IN POLITICS'

1 During the First World War in the German Empire a nail was hammered into objects, usually made of wood, and a donation given. These were called 'war nailings'. The money raised went to the victims of war and their families. 'The iron Hindenburg' in Berlin-Tiergarten was the largest nail figure and was erected in 1915.

2 The *Abitur* was and is comparable to A-levels, and allowed the holder to move on to university. The Lyzeum was a high school comparable to today's *Gymnasium* or grammar school. A Lyzeum was attended exclusively by girls.

'HITLER WAS SIMPLY JUST A NEW MAN'

1 Heinrich George (b. 9 October 1893 in Stettin; d. 25 September 1946 in Sachsenhausen Special Camp, Oranienburg) was a popular German actor even during the Weimar Republic. He was initially forbidden from working in the Nazi period, but he came to terms with the regime and acted in several propaganda films, including *Hitlerjunge Quex* (1933) and *Kolberg* (1945) as well as in the propaganda film *Jud Süß* (1940).

2 Attila Hörbiger (b. 21 April 1896, Budapest, Austria-Hungary; d. 27 April 1987 in Vienna, Austria) was an Austrian actor. From 1935 until 1937 and from 1947 until 1951 he played *Jedermann* (Everyman) at the Salzburg Festival. With his wife, Gattin Paula Wessely, he played in *Heimkehr*, an anti-Semitic propaganda film.

3 The 'Zeitfunk' department chiefly focused on events in Germany and Europe and at the fronts.

4   Eduard Roderich Dietze (b. 1 March 1909; d. 25 May 1960) was a German table-tennis player with Scottish roots, and worked as a Rundfunk reporter. In the 1936 Olympic Games he was the chief announcer for English-speaking Rundfunk. After the Second World War he was very involved in the development of television, and was later head reporter with Südwestfunk.

5   Rolf Waldemar Wernicke (b. 15 August 1903; d. 8 January 1953) was a German sports reporter. He reported in 1936 from the opening ceremony of the Olympic Games and the athletics competitions. But he also went on to report on central events such as Nazi rallies and, during the war, directly from the front.

6   Johannes Karl Holzamer (b. 13 October 1906; d. 22 April 2007) was a German philosopher and educator, and later director of the broadcaster ZDF. At the beginning of the Second World War, Holzamer was initially recruited into the Luftwaffe as a gunner and later delegated as a radio war reporter.

7   From 1934 many of the staff of the Reich Broadcasting Corporation in Berlin were arrested and banned from employment. These included prominent radio pioneers such as Julius Jänisch, Alfred Braun, Hans Bredow, Hans Flesch, Hermann Kasack, Friedrich Georg Knöpfke, Kurt Magnus, Franz Mariaux and Gerhart Pohl.

8   Ludwig Lesser (b. 1869 in Berlin; d. 1957 in Vallentuna/Sweden) was a Berlin landscape architect. After he was forbidden from working in the Nazi era he emigrated to Sweden in 1939 and was posthumously appointed honorary president of the German Gardening Association.

9   Heinrich Glasmeier (b. 1892 in Dorsten; presumed died in 1945) was a German broadcasting director, and after 1933 was the director of Westdeutscher Rundfunk in Cologne. In 1937 he became Reich Director of the whole German Rundfunk (Broadcasting Corporation), and from 1943 was employed as authorised representative of the Reich Propaganda Minister in occupied France.

'IT WAS A BIT OF AN ELITE'

1   The Berghof was Hitler's home near Berchtesgaden in Bavaria, Germany.

2 The economist Werner Naumann (b. 16 June 1909 in Guhrau, Silesia; d. 25 October 1982 in Lüdenscheid) was Secretary of State in the Reich Ministry of Popular Enlightenment and Propaganda and personal aide to Joseph Goebbels. In 1953 Naumann was involved in a conspiracy in which a group of former Nazis attempted to infiltrate the FDP (Free Democratic Party) in North Rhine Westphalia.

3 Kurt Frowein (b. 1914 in Wuppertal) became Joseph Goebbels's press attaché in 1940. In June 1943 he was promoted to Reich film producer (Reichsfilmdramaturg) and had considerable influence in the central control room of the media power of the Propaganda Ministry.

4 The White Rose was a resistance group led by students and a professor at the University of Munich. The core group was arrested by the Gestapo on 18 February 1943 and many of them, along with other members and supporters, were sentenced to death or imprisonment. The 20 July plot was an attempt by Claus von Stauffenberg and other conspirators to assassinate Adolf Hitler in 1944.

5 Between October 1941 and late March 1945, 50,000 Jews were deported from Berlin. When the Reich Propaganda Minister killed himself in May 1945, of the 160,000 Jews at the start of the Nazi dictatorship, only 8,000 still lived in Berlin. The last deportation train left Berlin on 27 March 1945 for Theresienstadt concentration camp – only six weeks before the end of the Third Reich.

6 Eva Löwenthal was deported from Berlin to Auschwitz on 8 November 1943, on transport number 46, and murdered there early in 1945.

7 Werner Paul Walther Finck (b. 2 May 1902 in Görlitz; d. 31 July 1978 in Munich) was a German cabaret performer, actor and author. In 1935 he was arrested and banned from employment for a year. To avoid being arrested again he volunteered for military service and later won the Iron Cross 2nd Class and the Winter Battle in the East Medal 1941–2.

8 Lída Baarová (b. 7 September 1914 as Ludmila Babková in Prague; d. 27 October 2000 in Salzburg). The Czech actress was the lover of Joseph Goebbels. The relationship was openly discussed early on, and the Propaganda Minister was prepared to divorce for the relationship. It was only when Hitler put his foot down that the

relationship came to an end, as he found the public debate undesirable at the time of the annexation of the Sudetenland – and besides, Goebbels's family was known as the Reich's model Nazi family.

9   In the Second World War, Südende in Berlin was almost entirely destroyed by Allied air raids. The crucial one came on the night of 23–24 August 1943 in a raid by a British bomber unit.

10 The lost battle for Stalingrad and the resulting destruction of the German 6th Army in early 1943 is considered the psychological turning point of the German–Soviet war that began in June 1941.

11 Konstantin von Schirmeister (b. 12 August 1901 in Mülhausen, Alsace; d. presumably after 1946) was a journalist, and from 1933 until 1945 as a state official was a high-ranking colleague of Joseph Goebbels in the Reich Ministry for Popular Enlightenment and Propaganda.

12 On 18 February 1943, Joseph Goebbels delivered a speech in the Sportpalast in Berlin, in which he called for 'total war'. The speech, which lasted around 109 minutes, is seen as a textbook example of Nazi propaganda.

13 The law on the Hitler oath for officials introduced on 20 August 1934 demanded the following oath of service: 'I swear: I will be loyal and obedient to the Führer of the German Reich and people, Adolf Hitler, respect the laws and conscientiously fulfil my official duties, so help me God.' Brunhilde Pomsel can't remember whether she had to deliver this oath verbatim as a member of the Ministry staff.

14 Richard Otte was a councillor and Joseph Goebbels's personal stenographer. He was involved in producing Joseph Goebbels's extensive diaries.

15 *Jud Süß* is an anti-Semitic National Socialist film by Veit Harlan, made in 1940.

16 Ferdinand Marian (b. 14 August 1902 in Vienna; d. 7 August 1946 in Pulling, Germany) was a popular Austrian actor in the 1930s. Joseph Goebbels personally demanded that Marian take the main role of the famous anti-Jewish Nazi propaganda film *Jud Süß*, which he had originally turned down.

17 Here Brunhilde Pomsel is referring to the film *Kolberg*. It was produced in 1943 under the auspices of Joseph Goebbels and was intended to boost the perseverance of the Germans during the last phase of the Second World War.

18 Universum Film Aktiengesellschaft, a major German film company that produced and distributed from 1917 to the end of the Second World War.

'LOYAL TO THE END'

1 Hans Georg Fritzsche (b. 21 April 1900 in Bochum; d. 27 September 1953 in Cologne) was a German journalist and held various offices in the Reich Ministry for Popular Enlightenment and Propaganda. After the battle for Berlin, on 2 May 1945, presumably as the most senior-ranking government official still in the city, Fritzsche signed the unconditional declaration of surrender for Berlin.

2 Günther Schwägermann (b. 24 July 1915 in Uelzen) served as adjutant to Joseph Goebbels from 1941. He attained the rank of an SS Hauptsturmführer. On 1 May 1945, during the last days of the battle for Berlin, he burned the corpses of Joseph and Magda Goebbels. Schwägermann successfully escaped from Berlin to West Germany. On 25 June 1945 he was imprisoned by the Americans, and released on 24 April 1947.

3 This refers to the army formed in April 1945 under Walther Wenck, the senior commander, in order to fight the battle of Berlin. It was the army with the youngest soldiers in the Wehrmacht, and very badly armed.

4 Adolf Hitler was born on 20 April 1889 in Braunau am Inn in Austria-Hungary.

5 Dr Herbert Collatz (b. 13 April 1899; d. 1945) was a senior councillor in the Reich Ministry of Popular Enlightenment and Propaganda. He shot himself and his family when the Russians invaded Berlin.

6 Johannes 'Hanne' Sobek (b. 18 March 1900 in Mirow; d. 17 February 1989 in Berlin) was a German footballer and trainer. He came to fame as a player with Hertha BSC, with whom he reached the finals of the German Championship six times in a row. At the end of his career as an active player, Sobek worked for Berliner Rundfunk as a reporter (1938–1945).

7 Vasily Ivanovich Chuikov (b. 12 February 1900 in Serebranye Prudy; d. 18 March 1982 in Moscow) was a much decorated

Russian general, commanding the 62nd Army from the battle of Stalingrad to the battle for Berlin in April–May 1945. After the war he was awarded the decoration of 'hero of the Soviet Union', and in 1955 he was made 'Marshall of the Soviet Union'.

'WE KNEW NOTHING'

1   Hanna Reitsch (b. 29 March 1912 in Hirschberg, Silesia; d. 24 August 1979 in Frankfurt am Main) was a very popular female test pilot. After Hermann Göring was relieved of all his offices by Hitler on 23 April 1945, on 26 April 1945 she flew his successor Robert Ritter von Greim to Berlin, arriving as the centre of the city was already occupied by the Red Army.

2   Martin Bormann (b. 17 June 1900 in Halberstadt; d. 2 May 1945 in Berlin) held important Party offices, finally becoming Director of the NSDAP Chancellery as Reich Minister, and a major confidant of Hitler. After escaping from the Führer's bunker early in May 1945 he was believed missing. It was only discovered in 1973 that he had killed himself on 2 May 1945. His skeleton was found when cables were being laid near the Lehrter Bahnhof station and subsequently identified.

'WHAT THE STORY OF GOEBBELS'S SECRETARY TEACHES US FOR THE FUTURE'

1   Paul Garbulski: '*Gib acht vor der Nazi-Sekretärin in dir*' ('Watch out for the Nazi secretary in you'), *VICE Magazin*, 17 August 2016, at: http://www.vice.com/de/read/sind-wir-nicht-alle-ein-biss-chen-pomsel, retrieved 28 December 2016.

2   Sven Felix Kellerhoff: '*Goebbels-Sekretärin will »nichts gewusst« haben*' ('Goebbels's secretary claims "to have known nothing"'), *Welt24*, 30 June 2016, at: https://www.welt.de/geschichte/zweiter-weltkrieg/article156710123/Goebbels-Sekretaerin-will-nichts-gewusst-haben.html, retrieved 28 December 2016.

3   Amnesty International: '*Hunderttausende Kurden im Süden der Türkei vertrieben*' ('Hundreds of thousands of Kurds driven out of southern Turkey'), Amnesty International, 6 December 2016,

at: https://www.amnesty.de/2016/12/6/hunderttausende-kurden-im-suedosten-der-tuerkei-vertrieben, retrieved 28 December 2016.

4 Sylke Gruhnwald and Alice Kohl: *'Die Toten vor Europas Toren'* ('The dead at Europe's gates'), *Neue Züricher Zeitung Online*, 2 April 2014, at: http://www.nzz.ch/die-toten-vor-europas-tueren-1.18272891, retrieved 28 December 2016.

5 Jean-Marc Manach: *'Ces gens-là sont morts, ce ne sont plus des migrants'* ('Those people are dead, they are no longer migrants'), in: *Le Monde diplomatique Online*, 31 March 2014, at: http://www.monde-diplomatique.fr/carnet/2014-03-31-morts-aux-frontieres, retrieved 28 December 2016.

6 Lutz Haverkamp, Markus Grabitz: '*10 000 Tote seit 2014 im Mittelmeer*' ('10,000 deaths in the Mediterranean since 2014'), in: *Der Tagespiegel Online*, 7 June 2016, at: http://www.tagesspiegel.de/politik/europaeische-union-und-die-fluechtlinge-10-000-tote-seit-2014-im-mittelmeer/13701608.html, retrieved 28 December 2016.

7 John Woodrow Cox: 'Let's party like it's 1933: Inside the alt-right world of Richard Spencer', in: *Washington Post Online*, 22 November 2016, at: https://www.washingtonpost.com/local/lets-party-like-its-1933-inside-the-disturbing-alt-right-world-of-richard-spencer/2016/11/22/cf81dc74-aff7-11e6-840f-e3ebab6bcdd3_story.html, retrieved 28 December 2016.

8 Richard Herzinger: *'Trump weiter zu unterschätzen ist selbstmörderisch'* ('Continuing to underestimate Trump is suicide'), in: *Welt24 Online*, 10 November 2016, at: https://www.welt.de/debatte/kommentare/article159392876/Trump-weiter-zu-unterschaetzen-ist-selbstmoerderisch.html, retrieved 28 December 2016.

9 Albrecht von Lucke: '*Trump und die Folgen: Demokratie am Scheideweg*' ('Trump and the consequences: democracy at the watershed'); *Blätter für deutsche und internationale Politik*, December 2016, pp. 5–9.

10 Timo Steppat: '*Wie Populisten durch Facebook groß werden*' ('How populists grow up through Facebook'), in: *Frankfurter Allgemeine Zeitung Online*, 11 November 2016, at: http://www.faz.net/aktuell/politik/inland/wie-facebook-po-pulisten-wie-trump-afd-und-pegida-gross-macht-14518781.html, retrieved 28 December 2016.

11 Hasnain Kazim: '*Ungefiltert FPÖ*' ('Austrian Freedom Party unfiltered'), in: *Spiegel Online*, 30 November 2016, at: http://www.spiegel.de/kultur/gesellschaft/rechte-medien-in-oesterreich-ungeltert-fpoe-a-1123653.html, retrieved 28 December 2016.

12 Edelman: 'Trust Barometer – Global Results', 2016, at: http://www.edelman.com/insights/intellectual-property/2016-edelman-trust-barometer/global-results, retrieved 28 December 2016.

13 The Southern Poverty Law Center: 'Ten Days After: Harassment and Intimidation in the Aftermath of the Election', November 2016, at: https://www.splcenter.org/20161129/ten-days-after-harassment-and-intimidation-aftermath-election#antimuslim, retrieved 28 December 2016.

14 Benedikt Peters: '*Gewalt gegen Ausländer geht nicht mehr weg*' ('Violence against foreigners isn't going away'), in: *Süddeutsche Zeitung Online*, 30 September 2016, at: http://www.sueddeutsche.de/politik/grossbritannien-gewalt-gegen-auslaender-geht-nicht-mehr-weg-1.3185999, retrieved 28 December 2016.

15 Jörg Winterbauer: '*Flüchtlingsfrage eskaliert in Form von körperlicher Gewalt*' ('Refugee question escalates in the form of physical violence'), in: *Welt24 Online*, 4 December 2015, at: https://www.welt.de/politik/ausland/article149607210/Fluechtlings-frage-eskaliert-in-Form-von-koerperlicher-Gewalt.html, retrieved 28 December 2016.

16 Giovanni di Lorenzo: '*Als München Nein sagte*' ('When Munich said no'), in: *Welt24 Online*, 2 December 2012, at: https://www.welt.de/print/wams/muenchen/article111757587/Als-Muenchen-Nein-sagte.html, retrieved 28 December 2016.

17 Emily Schultheis: 'Donald Trump: U.S. must start thinking about racial profiling', in: *CBS News Online*, 19 June 2016, at: http://www.cbsnews.com/news/donald-trump-after-orlando-racial-profiling-not-the-worst-thing-to-do, retrieved 28 December 2016.

18 Björn Höcke on 11 October 2016 during a speech in Osburg near Trier: http://www.iesstexte.de/2016/10/11/thueringer-afd-chef-will-menschen-entsorgen-empoert-das-irgend-wen, retrieved October 2016.

19 Joseph Goebbels: '*Der Nationalcharakter als Grundlage der Nationalkultur*' ('The national character as a foundation for national

culture', radio broadcast, 18 July 1932, at: https://archive. org/details/19320718JosephGoebbelsRundfunkVortragDer NationalcharakterAlsGrundlageDerNationalkultur11m43s_ 201611, retrieved 28 December 2016.

20 *Linken-Politiker erstattet Strafanzeige gegen Höcke* ('"Linke" politician files charges against Höcke'), in *Spiegel-Online*, 18 January 2017, at: http://www.spiegel.de/politik/deutschland/bjoern-hoecke-zentralrat-der-juden-ist-empoert-ueber-rede-des-afd-politikers-a-1130520.htmlwww.spiegel.de/politik/deutschland/bjoern-hoecke-zentralrat-der-juden-ist-empoert-ueber-rede-des-afd-politikers-a-1130520.html, retrieved 18 January 2017.

21 AFP/dsa | EurActiv.de: *'Le Pen attackiert Flüchtlingspolitik von "Kaiserin" Merkel'* ('Le Pen attacks the refugee policy of "Kaiserin" Merkel'), in: *EurActiv Online*, 17 September 2015, at: https://www.euractiv.de/section/eu-innenpolitik/news/le-pen-attackiert-fluchtlingspolitik-von-kaiserin-merkel, retrieved 28 December 2016.

22 The Millennial Dialogue Report, 2015, at: https:/www. millennialdialogue.com/media/1072/germany-italy-poland-report.pdf, retrieved 28 December 2016.

23 Edzard Reuter: *'Die Generation Y hat sich nie für Politik interessiert'* ('Generation Y has never been interested in politics'), in: *Zeit Online*, 2 March 2016, at: http://www.zeit.de/wirtschaft/2016-03/edzard-reuter-generation-y-ex-daimler-chekritik, retrieved 28 December 2016.

24 AG University Research, University of Konstanz: *'Entwicklung des politischen Habitus der Studierenden'* ('Development of the political habitus of students'), in: *Studierendensurvey*, News 40.3/06.12, at: https://cms.uni-konstanz.de/ag-hochschulforschung/news/ausgabe-36-41-2011-2012/, retrieved 16 January 2017.

25 Shell Deutschland Holding (ed.): *Jugend 2015* (Youth 2015) (Konzeption & Koordination: K. Hurrelmann, Gudrun Quenzel, TNS Infratest Sozialforschung), Frankfurt a. M. 2015.

26 Pew Research Center: 'Youth Engagement Falls; Registration Also Declines', in: *Pew Research Center Online*, 28 September 2012, at: http://www.people-press.org/2012/09/28/youth-engagement-falls-registration-also-declines/, retrieved 28 December 2016.

27 Paul Mason: '*DieWiederkehr der Dreißiger Jahre?*', *Blätter für deutsche und internationale Politik*, November 2016, pp. 31–2 ['Are we living through another 1930s?', *Guardian*, 1 August 2016].

28 Quoted from Roman Leick: '*Eine tief greifende Angst, dass das Überleben der Gesellschaft bedroht ist*' ('A deep-rooted anxiety that the survival of society is threatened'), in: *Spiegel Online*, 7 September 2016, at: http://www.spiegel.de/spiegel/zygmunt-bau-man-spiegel-gespraech-zu-uechtlingen-globalisierung-ter-ror-a-1111032.html, retrieved 28 December 2016.

29 Gerry Stoker, *Why Politics Matters: Making Democracy Work* (Palgrave Macmillan 2006), p. 88.

30 Ralf Melzer: '*Wie Rechtspopulismus funktioniert*' ('How right-wing populism works'), in: *Spiegel Online*, 2 October 2016, at: http://www.spiegel.de/politik/deutschland/rechtspopulismus-die-kraft-des-einfachen-gastbeitrag-ralf-melzer-a-1114191.html, retrieved 28 December 2016.

31 Von Lucke, op. cit.

32 Harald Schumann: '*Die Herrschaft der Superreichen*' ('The rule of the super-rich'), in: *Blätter für deutsche und internationale Politik*, December 2016, pp. 67–78.

33 Elisabeth Raether: '*Was macht die Autoritären so stark? Unsere Arroganz*' ('What makes authoritarians so strong? Our arrogance'), in: *Zeit Online*, 18 August 2016, at: http://www.zeit.de/2016/33/demokratie-klassenduenkel-rassismus-populismus, retrieved 28 December 2016.

34 Ipsos MORI: 'Research Highlights – December 2016', at: https://www.ipsos-mori.com/researchpublications/publications/1900/Ipsos-MORI-Research-Highlights-December-2016.aspx, retrieved 28 December 2016.

35 Frank Decker and Florian Hartlieb: '*Das Scheitern der Schill-Partei als regionaler Machtfaktor: Typisch für Rechtspopulismus in Deutschland?*' ('The failure of the Schill Party as a regional power facter: typical of right-wing populism in Germany'), in: Susanne Frölich-Steffen and Lars Rensmann (eds): *Populisten an der Macht. Populistische Regierungsparteien in West- und Osteuropa* (Populists in Power: Populist Government Parties in Western and Eastern Europe), Wien 2005, p. 117.

36 Heike Vowinkel: '*Die Angst am Ende eines Jahrhundertlebens*' ('The fear at the end of a century of life'), 2016, in: *Welt24 Online*, 4 October 2016, at: http://hd.welt.de/vermischtes/article158493992/Die-Angst-am-Ende-eines-Jahrhundertlebens. html, retrieved 28 December 2016.

37 Quoted from: '*Bastian Berbner und Amrai Coen: Trump muss sich erst mal informieren*' ('Bastian Berbner and Amrai Coen: Trump should do some research'), in: *Zeit Online*, 23 November 2016, at: http://www.zeit.de/politik/ausland/2016-11/henry-kissinger-inter-view-donald-trump-demokratie-usa-angst/seite-3, retrieved 28 December 2016.

INDEX

A NOTE ON THE AUTHORS

Brunhilde Pomsel was born in Berlin on 11 January 1911. After training to become a typist, she began a job in the news department of the state radio station in Berlin in 1933. Nine years later she joined the Propaganda Ministry as a secretary to Joseph Goebbels. Pomsel lived in Munich until her death in January 2017. She was 106 years old.

Thore D. Hansen is a German journalist and writer.

A NOTE ON THE TYPE

The text of this book is set in Perpetua. This typeface is an adaptation of a style of letter that had been popularised for monumental work in stone by Eric Gill. Large scale drawings by Gill were given to Charles Malin, a Parisian punch-cutter, and his hand-cut punches were the basis for the font issued by Monotype. First used in a private translation called 'The Passion of Perpetua and Felicity', the italic was originally called Felicity.